ABOUT THE AUTHOR

David Gardner is a writer and traveller. He is a published author of books and
scholarly articles, has a PhD in wine management, and now spends his time
writing about the magnificent landscapes and cultures through which he and his
wife travel.

ACKNOWLEDGEMENTS

I would like to thank my wife Wendy, for inspiring me to make this trip, for her wonderful company throughout our journey and finally, for her patience and skill in helping to edit the final manuscript.

An Italian Odyssey:

A journey through Tuscany & Sicily

Revised edition of
White Roads and Red Wine: A couple's journey through Italy

KNOX PUBLISHING
2021

CONTENTS

Chapter One: All Roads

Wendy and I had been planning the trip for the past twelve months and had been looking forward to this day for far too long. It was the second marriage for us both, which had taken place only a year beforehand. Wendy's daughter was doing her final year at school when we married, so the house was in virtual lockdown for the remainder of that year.

On top of that, my ageing mother had been in and out of hospital over this time, and our combined children were still getting used to their parents being married to someone else. We were all handling it relatively well, with only minor hiccups and rarely a meltdown. But Wendy and I were reaching overload and desperately needed time away and time together. This trip, therefore, was a delayed and very much extended honeymoon, one that would last for months!

Roma

After a 14-hour flight to Doha and another six on to Rome, we arrive exhausted at the first of our destinations. Rome's Leonardo da Vinci Airport is loud, friendly, passionate, chaotic. We breeze through immigration and customs with barely a glance from the officials. So much for airports' heightened security in the wake of recent terror activity. There was an expectation of considerable delay through baggage and person searches, multiple questions and suspicious looks directed at each passenger. But not here in Italy apparently. Immigration officials chat with each other while absent-mindedly waving passengers through gates. It's wonderful for us after such a long flight but I hate to think who might be getting into the country. The airport "express" to our apartment is delayed by 50 minutes because of an ambiguous strike involving Alitalia.

When, at last we climb aboard our transport, we're in for one of the most frightening experiences of our lives. Our driver seems to have assumed that we would all like to join him in his apparent death wish. Wendy, who is a notoriously nervous passenger, spends the fifty-minute journey with her head down and hands covering her eyes in an effort to avoid passing out. We are in a battered old mini-van and I stupidly didn't bother clipping my seatbelt in as we took off. Now I can't stay on the seat long enough to remedy the situation.

It's exactly like being in a rollercoaster at a fun park, except the ride never ends. Our driver delights in going as fast as he can between each set of lights and even better, squeezing past red lights before oncoming traffic closes the gap. The narrower the road, the faster he drives and for extra fun, takes both hands off the wheel to light a cigarette while approaching a corner.

The roads, or laneways, I should say, are almost all cobble stones so that as we accelerate to 100kph in a tiny backstreet (because they are all tiny backstreets) the mini-bus feels like it will split open with the shaking. The four of us who were foolish enough to get on board are bouncing around, trying for dear life to simply stay on the seat. I hear an "Oh dear God" from behind me and turn to see the elderly female passenger looking very pasty, also with eyes closed. But it gets worse. These little streets are choked with traffic, all moving at the same speed and all attempting to change lanes simultaneously. They seem to share our death wish. Then there is one more problem – the pedestrians. People are strolling aimlessly along these lanes, seemingly oblivious to what's coming at them. As our bus hurtles along, they lazily move aside by the merest of inches to avoid our front bumper. It is done without a care in the world. Our driver never shows any intention in slowing as he approaches them and they show no intention of caring.

The normal rules of behaviour just don't apply. People are driving with a recklessness you rarely see back home. Then, when I think there's no more road rules to be flouted, our driver decides he is going to cross four lanes of heavy, fast moving traffic in order to get to a little laneway on the other side. Two lanes travelling north and two south with bumper-to-bumper traffic and he decides he's going to cross now. Wendy and I look at each other and I spot a thin line of sweat on her brow. I break into a giggle at the ludicrousness of our situation. But the driver pushes his way through and somehow, miraculously, we don't hit anything. Traffic just swerves around us and goes on its way. A couple of drivers yell abuse and our driver yells back as he pushes the accelerator further into the floor. After almost an hour of this he suddenly slams on the breaks and the van shudders to a stop. Our driver turns to us with a smile and says; "We are here". Wendy lets out a small groan and rises shakily to her feet. I feel like we've had all our holiday adventures in one action-packed hour.

A city of contrasts and contradictions
Rome first strikes you as a city of wonderful and relentless contrasts. It is of course part of the European Union. Yet within a community that has been criticised for its weight of rules and unnecessary regulations, Italians seem to take pride in flouting every rule they can identify. While the rest of the EU often adheres to rigid formulas of behaviour, whether political, social, economic, or legal, Italians act on a whim.

Cars are parked wherever a space is found, front in, back in and wedged end on between two others. They ride their beloved mopeds while talking on mobiles. I actually saw one fellow steering his moped with his elbows while messaging on his phone. Even more astounding was that as he did so, he rode past a stationary police car with two officers. Although they clearly saw him, they kept chatting with no thought of giving chase.

Despite their road behaviour, however, Italians are some of the friendliest people you will find. Despite the size and congestion of Rome, where locals are confronted by tourists in relentless waves, there is nothing these people won't do for you. You ask directions and instead of pointing, or turning away as many of my fellow Australians might do, they will ask you to follow them and walk you to your destination. This happened to us on a number of occasions. And, while we felt a bit strange walking with a stranger, we appreciated the kindness shown.

Romans also appear passionate about life, often tackling tasks with a sense of urgency and haste, yet usually role up late for appointments. When they announce that they'll meet you at a particular spot at 10.am, they really mean "at some stage during the day". They love their relaxation and will idly stop in the middle of an errand to share a drink with a friend at the local bar. They are passionate about doing *nothing* when the mood takes them. Their emphasis is on family and friends. There is a strong belief in family and community support, in maintaining bonds of loyalty and interdependence. Archaeologist Francis Pryor tells us in his book – Britain AD - that the Roman sense of 'community' dates back as far as the late Iron Age.

Yet they are fiercely independent, protesting at all kinds of infringements. There is a widespread rejection of CCTV cameras. There is a rejection of directives from government if they interfere with personal choice. There is a rejection of practices that upset the community equilibrium. Only last year, a vote to reform a dysfunctional and commonly abused constitution, to introduce a more transparent electoral system came back with a resounding "NO" vote. Apparently, Italians saw this initiative as unnecessary meddling in their lives.

Yet you can't help loving these people. I love the way they throw out things they don't like. I love the way they grasp life and shake it by the collar. I love the way *they* love life; the energy they inject into the most normal of daily functions. Monotony does not seem to enter their day.
****

Unrolling history

It is hard not to soak up the history embedded in every Roman street and building. It's intoxicating. History overtakes you wherever you walk along these cobblestone streets. Some of the stones were laid as much as 2,000 years ago, so you can only imagine who and what has gone before you.

The history of Rome is well known to most of us, having endured several years of ancient history classes in high school. The Roman Empire's structures, language, architecture and culture still underpin many of our political and social models.Today, Rome is a vibrant, busy, and highly commercial city with a population of over two and a half million people. It is the largest city of a national economy that ranks third in the European Union. So, by any standard it's important. But its historical significance still resonates globally and inspires scholars and tourists alike. It sits on the beautiful, fast-flowing River Tiber. Its beginnings can be traced back to around 700BCE. At its most powerful Rome dominated Europe and was virtually untouchable economically and militarily. We forget how much of our current language owes its legacy to Rome. Languages such as Italian, Portuguese, Spanish and French derive to a greater or lesser degree from the Roman language of Latin. It was also the first successful republic and inspired many modern-day republics including that of the United States of America.

But it influenced far more than just our language and political systems. So much more of our current knowledge – letters, history, technology and commerce – is derived directly or indirectly from the great Roman Empire. In many ways Rome represented the beginning of the modern world. And being once the greatest power on earth it also devised one of the world's largest and cashed-up religious institutions - Catholicism – a religion that still controls 98% of Italy's citizens and a billion worldwide.

Taking it all in
This morning we decide to stroll through the centre of the city. Right before us, in the middle of two major roadways with hundreds of cars and pedestrians, is an archaeological site that dates back 1,800 years. It is the Largo di Torre Argentina, a site that includes the remains of four Roman Republican temples, as well as Pompey's Theatre. Amusingly, it is also a cat sanctuary, with a 'no-kill' law for homeless cats. You can tell. There are cats wandering and lazing in the sun right through the site – hundreds of them!

Although it doesn't rank with sites such as the Pantheon, the Spanish Steps, the Roman Forum, the Piazza Navona, or the Colosseum, I found it every bit as captivating. The fact that it's not noted as a tourist destination but simply occupies a modest space in the middle of busy roadways and shops somehow adds to its aura. In fact, archaeological sites are things that Rome has in abundance. While I have tried to focus on the influence Rome has had on me personally, it would be remiss to brush past the famous, albeit tourist sites that make up so much of this city's incredible history.

Indeed, the Colosseum and Spanish Steps and Pantheon are marvels in their own right and allow modern day visitors to gain some small insight into what made Rome the unrivalled empire it once was. I remember the first time I laid eyes on the Colosseum in our manic airport transfer into the city. For a moment my breath caught in my chest. We turned a corner and there it was, right in front of us. It's difficult to describe the effect it first has on you. Most of all I felt a rush of adrenaline, seeing an almost perfect historic monument, a monument that may well be the finest example of Roman architecture ever created, one about which I had heard and learnt so much over my lifetime, sitting there as plain as day in front of me. All I could think was "Oh my God".

The Colosseum was built almost two thousand years ago, between AD 70 and AD 80 and was on such a grand scale for its time that it takes your mind a little while to adjust. There were eighty separate entrances and space for 50,000 spectators as well as thirty-six trapdoors to cells beneath, where slaves and wild animals were kept awaiting their turn in the arena. The building was designed purely for entertainment, entertainment for the emperor, his wives, other nobles and the Roman masses and by our sensitive standards today, it boasts a fairly dark and grizzly legacy. Over half a million people and more than a million animals, involved in a sport of killing for the enjoyment of their onlookers, lost their lives in this arena. Humans against humans, and humans against animals fought until the death. It was a national sport similar to our football games today, but even more brutal. In fact, one of the main reasons this sport came to an end five hundred years later was simply because it was becoming more and more difficult to find and capture enough wild animals. Some species were reduced to virtual extinction levels purely through the Roman Empire's penchant for watching them battle against humans.

From the Colosseum you take a half-hour walk to the very long flight of Spanish Steps, steps, which were funded by the French and built by Italians in the 1720s.

So really, there is nothing Spanish about them. But they were intended as a cultural meeting place for great artists to gather and discuss their works and gain mutual inspiration. This, they have remained, and over the centuries have drawn millions of people from all corners of the globe, tourists, artists, researchers, pilgrims, all coming for their own reasons and gaining their own little bit of inspiration. Back in 2007, a rather drunken fellow even climbed into his Toyota and drove down these marvellous steps, damaging many of them and possibly not gaining much inspiration. He did, however, attract the law and paid dearly for his adventure.

I suppose a site that has the most profound effect on me is the Pantheon. Built as a temple to the Gods, the Pantheon epitomises elegance and symmetry. And, although constructed 2,000 years ago, its beauty and perfection remain an architectural wonder even today. When we first visited the Pantheon, it was close to midday and the crowds were out, a myriad of ubiquitous tour groups, as well as hundreds of other visitors like us. We waited to go inside, past the two military personnel at the entrance, with their automatic weapons, staring sternly at each of us as we filtered through.

Once inside the cavernous building your eyes are immediately drawn upwards to the poetically domed ceiling. It was engineered in such a way that the very centre of the ceiling is punctured by a perfectly circular hole (known as the eye of the Pantheon) through which light streams at different angles depending on the time of day. It is like a solid torchlight that illuminates various points on the floor below and highlights the incredible sculptures along the interior walls. As the sun progresses across the sky, the light not only changes direction, but also colour, moving through a spectrum from bright white at midday to deep mauves and pinks, lilacs and oranges as the evening gains dominance. It's quite mesmerising and as I look around, almost every one of the people crowding inside have their faces turned upwards to this magnificent feat of engineering. Even today, it remains the largest unsupported dome in the world, and to understand that this was built two millennia ago is to realise that we too often underestimate the skills of those who come before us.

The Pantheon is said to be the best-preserved monument in all of Rome, surviving wars, raids, climate and two thousand years of time, but apart from its ability to withstand the elements, it is above all, a thing of exquisite beauty. Wendy and I have a need to experience it one more time. Our next visit is in the early morning, a walk through the empty streets from our apartment. When we arrive at the Piazza della Rotonda, in which the Pantheon stands, it too is blessedly empty. It is too early for the Pantheon's opening, although the two military personnel with their associated hardware are again on guard.

We don't need to be inside. We simply wanted to see this magnificent historical statement without crowds, when the early morning light plays across its historic structure. And what a sight it is! The entire edifice is bathed in a vibrant lilac as sunrise casts its enchanting spell across the piazza. There is no-one here to appreciate it except Wendy and me, and the two soldiers, and I suppose that makes it just a little more special. We stand and take in this splendour for considerable time, before finally heading back to breakfast and our already best memory of the day.

***

In the Quirinale district of Rome, along with thousands of other tourists, you will come across the Trevi Fountain, one of the city's oldest sources of fresh water. The first time we visit it is too early, with the Fountain being closed to tourists while being cleared of tossed coins from the previous day. I foolishly bypass the fence to approach the serene monument. Immediately I am stopped by a police officer, emerging from I don't know where. She lets me know in no uncertain terms that I need to wait. We decide to go back for breakfast and come again later in the day. On our return the piazza has transformed into a moving tide of people all surging towards the fountain with cameras and selfi-sticks in hand. It s not even close to tourist season so I can't begin to imagine the crowds in summer. The city has some of the most popular tourist sites on offer and unless you visit these at dawn or late at night you will have to share the sites with masses of people.

There must be a dozen separate tour groups here and more are crowding into the piazza behind us. They all want to throw their coins in for that special wish. The wish is of returning to Rome and will only be fulfilled if you first turn your back to the Fountain and use your right hand tossing a coin over your left shoulder. I'm not sure why it is such a complicated manoeuvre, but you can imagine the chaotic state with hundreds of people attempting this simultaneously and then pushing others aside to get the perfect photo.

The Trevi Fountain began life as a natural fresh water spring all the way back in 19BC when legend has it that thirsty soldiers were taken there to refresh themselves. Of course, it was not actually a fountain then and wasn't constructed in its Baroque style until 1762. It is built of a beautiful smooth, white/blue stone, said to have been dragged from the Tiber River. While it is claimed to be one of the most popular sites in all of Rome and was one of Wendy's MUST DO activities here, the Fountain just didn't grab me in the same way that other sites have. I did respectfully stand and take photos with everyone else and *did* notice the rapture in other's faces, but I just couldn't quite bring myself to get excited about it.

Myths and Reality

As with any tourist destination, there are an abundance of historical and cultural myths that inhabit Rome's landscape. A number of 'facts' are designed to fit in nicely with the legend and where certain facts become inconvenient, they are usually left out. One fact the Romans would like to forget is the non-existent relationship between the Spanish Steps and Spain. Another is the Roman claim of Latin as their official language. While they did speak a form of Latin, it was a base and uncultured form and not the classical language that has been handed down over the centuries.

A fact which is also glossed over for Hollywood movies and best-selling historical novels, is that a significant number of Roman gladiators, that most masculine of ancient warrior, were in fact women, many of whom showed more prowess than their male counterparts. But perhaps the most obviously inverted fact is the modern saying that "All roads lead to Rome". The original saying was that "All roads lead *from* Rome". The modern-day inversion does not give sufficient credit to the enormously influential stretch of the Empire or its global interests in an age before *globalisation* was even a concept. The fact that "all roads led from Rome" underlines this city as the hub of hegemonic, centralised power from which orders were taken as far away as England, Carthage, and Africa.

Minimisation

A major issue of a city as old as Rome is the width of the streets and particularly, its laneways. In fact, in the historical centre the lanes are so narrow and winding that traffic is confined to tiny *smart* cars, and fiat 500s that you could pick up and carry if you needed to, as well as thousands of mopeds. The ubiquitous moped is ridden by all, from the young to the very old. Wrinkled grandmothers are seen zipping between cars and pedestrians on their way to and from their *late* appointments. Each street has long rows of these mopeds parked along each side and their tiny lawn-mower engines are heard night and day. But, like other forms of transport here, there appear to be no rules. They weave in and out of pedestrians, on footpaths, between cars, against traffic and through busy markets. There are often two or three riders riding astride, chatting as they go.

Not so bright

On a darker note, there are many homeless in Rome. They line these cobbled streets asking for money and food. They are here from earliest morning until late every night. And they can be easily seen from Rome's grandest premise a mere half-mile across the river. Some of these homeless are Gypsies, others are of North African descent, a number of them disabled and afflicted in a myriad of ways. There are, at last count, almost 8,000 disabled homeless people now in Rome. They are a small but critical component of the total number of homeless, which are estimated at around 150,000 and growing.

There is also growing resentment by some residents to these people. There are demands that the local and provincial governments *do* something about the homeless – the implication being that they should be removed. In 2008, a national survey on the question of what should be done found that 68% of Italians wanted all Gypsies and homeless refugees expelled from the country. Others have called for even more severe measures such as fingerprinting these poor devils for "identity purposes". There are, of course, also professional beggars, who see it as occupation, setting up their blankets carefully each morning for a pre-determined duration. They select the most advantageous spots along well-known tourist routes. This category tends to confound the issues before government, as well as the sympathies of fellow residents. Whatever category of homeless these people fulfil; it is a relentlessly miserable and demoralising way to spend one's life.

This is highlighted further when you pass them on your way to the Vatican. This collection of palaces is housed within Vatican City, which, in terms of geographical footprint, is the smallest sovereign nation on the planet. Per capita, it is also one of the wealthiest. Inside Vatican City, all power – economic, cultural, religious, legislative and legal – resides with one person, the Pope. The entire nation is less than half a square kilometre. As for the collection of palaces, however, it is immense, with more than one thousand rooms and apartments. It can be seen from any corner of Rome and St Peter's Basilica is a landmark and visual checking point in navigating the city.

The exterior of the Vatican is stunning, but inside it's even more mind-numbingly so. Many things today are labelled as priceless. But the artefacts of the Vatican are *truly* priceless. It is simply not possible to place a value on its possessions or buildings. Much of it is beyond normal imagination and beyond anything I have ever seen. In fact, after several hours of wandering through the halls it becomes so overwhelming that it ceases to register. The magnificence is absolute. What this magnificence *does* underline is the unsurpassed power and wealth of the Catholic Church over its long history. No other single institution has wielded such enormous power over believers and non-believers alike. The roots of this power can be traced back to the early second millennium.

From the 1100s for a period of close to six hundred years, the Church orchestrated a monopoly on knowledge. With a great percentage of the population being illiterate and unable to access information readily, the Catholic Church placed itself as "protector" of all current and historical knowledge. From this it drew immense power. Further, as this power grew monarchs became more "attuned" to the Church's needs and wishes, often signing these wishes into law. Vast estates and tracts of land were routinely granted to the Church and the right to extract "rent" from those occupying them. In fact, at the height of its power, as the only Church for much of the medieval period, it owned more than a third of all land in Western Europe.

Today, the accumulated collection of wealth in the Vatican is beyond that of the Medicis or Rothschilds, or in fact, any other single collection in the world. You walk through room after room of ancient Egyptian artefacts, gold statues, Italian collections, marble ornaments and furniture, silver busts, priceless paintings, murals, hangings of all description, mosaic floors. The sheer, unadulterated opulence is stunning. It may also be a little concerning. This potent symbol of the Church's power and wealth, in sharp contrast to the Church's original mandate, is surrounded by Rome's most distressing symbol of impoverishment. Homeless people line the pavement on each side of the roadway all the way to Vatican City. Their poverty and degradation is as obvious as the Vatican's extreme grandeur. The two, side by side represent a worrying contradiction that doesn't bear too close an inspection.

Take Two

On a somewhat brighter note, our apartment for this trip is a mere 200 metres from the famous Campo de Fiori Markets, housed in a piazza that dates back to the early middle-ages. Fortunately, the Piazza's current activities are far more enjoyable and uplifting than its original use, which was as a place of public execution. The markets are usually open from 8.am to 3.pm every day and are a hive of activity, noise and colour. There are flower stalls, leather stalls, fruit and vegetable stalls, butchers, purveyors of cheese and olives, wine, olive oil, woven products, nuts, pasta and in fact, most things you might like in your kitchen. The produce is incredibly fresh and ranges in price from dirt cheap to a bit more than reasonable. The atmosphere is exhilarating. There are people everywhere, locals and tourists alike, haggling with vendors while drinking their morning coffees. It is wonderful to just be a part of this, to be among the rapid flow of local commerce and bartering.

Each morning we wander down to buy our supplies for that night's dinner, plus of course, a gelato to have on the way back. It is an activity that provides us with just a small glimpse into the local culture. The gelatos, by the way, are something beyond your wildest dreams. I don't know what the Italians do differently but nothing even comes close to them back home. Suffice it to say, we over-indulge.

Then, again in late afternoon or evening, we will wander back to these markets to sit at one of the many popular, outdoor bars that ring the piazza. We sip beers and listen to the local musicians as they serenade punters. Is there any better way to spend your time? These people know how to extract the most from life and this ritual becomes a highlight of our day. Locals flock here each afternoon to relax with friends after the workday. Unlike many cultures, they don't seem to take themselves or their daily duties too seriously, always leaving time to enjoy each other and a lifestyle that focuses on friends and family.

Food and wine

The food in Rome is a feast for the eyes and taste buds. It is parochial but if you like Italian food, then you will be delighted with the variety and quality. Numerous markets and Co-ops offer all the local cuisines that Romans indulge in daily. Locally grown tomatoes, truffles, mushrooms, olives, cheeses, strawberries, aubergines, peperoni, courgettes, grapes, and spinach. In fact, every fruit and vegetable you can imagine is on offer. Labels on these foods tell you where they were grown and when they were harvested/prepared. The majority of produce is locally grown so there is little deterioration during transportation. The other advantage is that much of the food is ordered in small quantities, so that unlike western supermarkets, it isn't returned to cold storage each night and then brought out again the next day. This ensures a freshness that we are unused to. A really pleasant surprise when food shopping is the cost. We were expecting Italy, and particularly Rome, to be on the expensive side. If you keep away from the tourist hotspots and instead visit Co-ops and markets in backstreets, the prices of fruit, vegetables, meat and dairy are, on average, about half what we would pay back home in Australia. Whereas we might pay AUD$4 for a 400g punnet of strawberries for example, here in Rome we have been paying the equivalent of AUD$1.50 for a kilo, less than half the price for more than double the amount. It is a foodie's heaven.

We notice that the locals tend to shop for each meal rather than weekly, and why not when the food is brought in daily? Authenticity is kept at the forefront of our mind as we peruse shelves, selecting delicacies for the night ahead. I hadn't realised that grocery shopping could be so satisfying, but when you are in the midst of such delicious, fresh, local fare and you can buy the whole meal's ingredients for less than ten euros, there is a degree of pleasure that transcends normal shopping experiences. And it's just as well the Italian produce is so good, because if you're looking for a restaurant meal, you should not expect an eclectic range of cuisines. Search as we might in the historic centre, there was little sign of Vietnamese, Korean, Thai, Lebanese, French, South American, or for that matter, any other international cuisine on offer. It was Italian only. Usually excellent Italian, but very little else. If you land in the middle of New York City, London, Singapore, Sydney or Berlin you can choose from just about any cuisine you care to think of, but not here.

The wines, which particularly attracted my attention, are also cheap by our standards, with very good Chiantis on offer for 8-10 euros. You realise what a large wine producer Italy is, with such an extensive range on offer at every price point. In fact, Italy currently ranks as the world's largest wine producer by volume, producing approximately 33% of the world's consumption. But again, the parochial marketing is obvious as you scan shelf upon shelf of Italian-only wines. There are almost no French, Spanish, US or Australian wines to be found anywhere. It seems that these people just prefer their own product. Although Italy is part of the EU, this seems a very un-EU type of cultural position.

Nevertheless, you want for nothing as your taste buds delight in the flavours. Italians love their food and wine. The preparation and cultivation of truly local products gives meaning to their lives and their way of life. Food is not a convenience or a simple hunger quencher to these people. It is part of their daily ritual, part of the fabric that binds their communities and families.

According to Italian chef Gorgio Locatelli, how a dish should be cooked and the appropriate sauce and pasta type for that dish is very serious business. He tells the story of when he was growing up and the deep mistrust his parents held for a neighbouring family simply because they added parsley to their minestrone soup. Such cultural and social delineations are hard to imagine unless food is embedded in your values. In my own country there may be a delineation between families who eat at McDonalds and those who prefer a wider selection of fare, but that is about as far as our food culture goes. It is simply not an intimate component of our national psyche as it is here.

Swimming in Lights

Another delight is taking late night walks along the eerily lit but majestic Tiber River. This historic river winds its way through the city in a broad, rapidly flowing sweep. It has done this for millennia, representing a powerfully liquid expression of the city's history. The events it has witnessed, the lives it has entered and transformed and the passage of time through which it has flowed create a narrative that is both dramatic and timeless. The Tiber is one of Europe's largest rivers, coursing through more than two hundred and fifty miles from beginning to end. Its history is as varied as the Italian's themselves. Beginning life as a major arterial waterway for traffic – usually commerce and trade – to a natural defence line, a military centre for centuries, and then a naval base during the Punic wars. It was originally named *Albulula* because of its clear white colour tones, before being renamed after the King of Alba Longa – Tiberinus – who drowned in its waters. In the 6th century BCE, the river's main function was more that of an open sewer than a river, waiting until the early Roman Empire to be cleansed and connected to their bathing houses. Like so much of Rome and its inhabitants, this river inspires. Its beauty at night is ethereal. City lights dance across its surface, reflecting in layers of silver, and scarlet and flickering green. It flows in silence and grace soothing you after a hectic day traversing the city beyond. Another contrast and another enchanting aspect of this unique city.

To me, Rome is many things. It's chaotic, exciting, charming, romantic, but can also be uncaring and sometimes contradictory. Above all, however, Rome is a city that touches your soul, and will invigorate the weariest of travellers with its wonder and passion.

Chapter Two: Ah Chianti!

It is with sadness that we leave our beautiful little apartment in the Campo de Fiori. On a narrow, Medieval, cobblestone street in the midst of a Roman community, with the type of drama and excitement that only the Italians can deliver, it brought a new dimension to our lives. I think we will return to this corner of the world often to indulge our appetite for all the passion and history that this city continues to deliver.

For the next stage of our adventure, we head to the train station and deliverance to an altogether more elegant version of Italian life. Any who are familiar with the Australian rail system will share my scepticism of "efficient and comfortable" rail travel. So when we decided to catch the train from Rome to Florence I was somewhat dubious. Arriving at Rome's main railway station it is slightly disconcerting to see armoured personnel carriers and soldiers with semi-automatic guns lining the entrance. They look serious and intimidating. I smile as I walk past but get a stern nothing in response. Entering the station, I immediately understand why it is guarded. Rome's main station is about four times the size and infinitely busier than our Central train station in Sydney. This seems odd given that the Roman population is 4.3 million, roughly the same as our own city of Sydney. Obviously, these people are a lot keener on public transport than us. I have rarely seen crowds like it, but everyone appears to be moving efficiently. There are no bottle-necks and huge electronic notice boards on every wall provide complete information on train departures and arrivals, platform numbers, train numbers, and times. I was not expecting this.

We have a leisurely coffee before strolling over to Platform 2, Departure Gate 9929. Our Very Fast Train is waiting. There are no such trains in Australia. At every election for the past twenty years Australia's Very Fast Train plan has been rolled out and advertised heavily by each party, both trying to outdo the other with promised lower costs and better services. After the election, these promises quietly disappear, not to be heard of again for another four years. So, this train is a bit of a novelty. It's more like boarding a commercial airliner than a train. We have allocated seats, which are large, leather and comfortable. We have an on-board entertainment system as well as free wifi, things that are simply unheard of on our train network back home. My scepticism is quickly evaporating.

Our train glides out of the station and within minutes two hostesses come down the aisle offering complimentary food and juices. The train is smooth and quiet and we are travelling at what feels like a reasonable speed but nothing too fast; that is until I look up at the on-board speedometer, which is showing 260kmph. I then look out of the window to see cars, trees and houses blurring past at an incredible pace. The quiet smoothness in our carriage has successfully camouflaged the speed at which we're traveling. The trip is a dream and is over before I can make any real progress on the electronic letter I'm writing. What's more, we left and arrived at exactly the times advertised on the schedule. I now understand the crowds using Italian transport networks. Why wouldn't they?

From what I understand, Italy's economy is in a whole load of trouble. Its growth rate is one of the lowest in the EU, unemployment is high, the housing market is depressed, public debt to equity ratio is frightening at close to 150%, and the flow of capital has declined significantly. Yet their train and bus systems run efficiently and at low cost to the consumer. There is a lesson in there somewhere.

Dreaming in Stone

Our connecting bus is already waiting for us and again, leaves on time. As we trundle, far too fast along the uncomfortably narrow road from Florence to Greve in Chianti, we pass through countryside that can be described as 'scrubby' at best. From the moment we leave Florence, the appeal of the landscape has continued to deteriorate. I'm trying to convince myself that despite this unpleasant surprise we will somehow manage to occupy ourselves and find walking routes away from these treacherous little roads. Wendy and I begin to exchange apprehensive glances, hers with a hint of resentment. After all, it was me who organised this section of the holiday and convinced her that two weeks in a medieval village, removed quite effectively from normal civilisation, would be a delightfully relaxing interlude in the holiday. Her look says, "perhaps it would, but not in this type of landscape, and by the way, thanks for wasting two weeks of my holiday".

Our moods darken further as we pass through non-descript villages that offer no more than dusty streets and sterile scenery. After thirty minutes of this we are positively morose. I can feel Wendy's antipathy building and know that I'm not going to come out of these two weeks at all well. She keeps asking in a slightly menacing way where on earth we are going to walk, followed by; "If we can't walk, what the heck are we going to do?" I mumble something inarticulate and take an urgent interest in anything that is away from her line of sight.

Then quite abruptly, the scenery begins to change as our bus starts to climb, and climb, and climb. The 'scrubbiness' and drab villages disappear to be replaced by open spaces, wisteria, countless cherry blossoms of pink, white and mauve. Olive groves and vineyards emerge on both sides and stretch to the horizon. Architecture becomes decidedly Tuscan looking and large villas are seen dominating distant hills. The static electricity surrounding Wendy is noticeably less potent. She even flashes me a faint smile. My mood instantly lifts. I'm not sure how the landscape improved so dramatically so quickly, but I feel that at least the marriage counsellor has been postponed for a bit.

And so, after just short of an hour travelling, we arrive in the picturesque Chianti town of Greve (amusingly pronounced gravy). Greve has a population of only 14,000 people, but it has a vibrant, energetic feel that gives the impression of a much larger town. It is commonly viewed as the gateway to Chianti. The town is typically Tuscan, with a building code that mandates houses and apartments have cream or light-yellow walls with burnt orange terracotta roofs. There's a pretty little stream flowing through the centre of town. The many shops, which line each side of the main street, are tiny and busy. As with most Tuscan towns there is a central piazza where the locals congregate and where restaurants have their outdoor dining areas. This piazza – Piazza Matteotti - is actually the original site of the town, which was established in the 11th century. It's an invitingly pretty area, with arched 'loggias' surrounding the square to provide shade in the hot summer months.

The streets of Greve are of course the Italian brand of narrow, and as usual, the cars are made to fit. Almost everyone is driving tiny Fiats, Peugeots, Renaults, Smart Cars, and Mopeds. Some still drive the traditional Italian three-wheelers – Piaggio Apes - that look like they might tip over if they hit a large stone. Old men with grim faces are usually crouched and cramped inside, puttering their way through town with fresh produce or vine cuttings in the back tray. The place has a very "local" feel to it. Our excitement levels rise. I'm pretty sure Wendy is feeling much happier with my choice, as she reaches across and clasps my hand – a positive sign for our lengthy stay ahead.

The host from whom we are renting our villa has kindly offered to pick us up at the bus stop and transport us back to the residence. Our medieval village of Montefioralle is only a mile from the town of Greve, but it is a mile steeply up hill. Our host is a friendly, talkative young mother of two who unashamedly practices her English on us all the way to the villa. She is a local, whose family owns a prime vineyard in the area as well as two villas in Montefioralle and a house in Florence. They're obviously not short of cash. She runs through the few local restaurants and special points of interest on the way, fills us in on the Saturday markets, as well as the best way to get between each of the surrounding villages. Her little girl sits quietly in the baby seat, eyeing us with suspicion. We are obviously an unwelcome surprise that has upset her routine and her familiar ride with mum.

Winding our way up to the tiny but gorgeous village high on its hill, we delight in the rows of olive trees bordering the road and the green valley stretching out beyond. Many of the olive trees have workers perched high in their branches pruning them for the next season. They wave or tip their hats as we pass. Trees border vineyards on the far side, which sweep across hills and down into shallow valleys for miles. It's a truly enchanting sight and I realise that Wendy and I have been subconsciously smiling the entire way. Chianti is already more than we hoped for.

The thousand-year-old village of Montefioralle is constructed from the local cream/burnt orange stone that looks like it will easily last another thousand years. I feel tears at the back of my eyes as I look on to what is possibly the most exquisite setting of a village I have ever seen. The census describes the population of Montefioralle as; twenty-one singles, including fourteen males and seven females; thirty-two married people; one person legally separated; two divorced; and four widows/widowers. Such a quaint description and such a tiny community. The total population is recorded as sixty persons and from what we gather they form a very close-knit group.

The village also seems to be largely ancestral. There are multiple generations living here and although houses and apartments are put up for sale occasionally, many seem to be kept in the family, passed from parents to children. This enhances the communal atmosphere. Everyone knows everyone else and has done so for a long time. This way the history of the village continues to live and remain relevant to each inhabitant. People leave their medieval doorways and walk the cobbled streets that countless generations of ancestors have done before them, wearing the same tracks and treading the same stones beneath. It is quite evocative to stroll along these lanes, knowing that people have been walking them to and from their daily business, with their own needs and wants, problems and challenges, for almost a thousand years. There is no possibly greater history lesson.

Montefioralle is recorded as the most ancient of all villages in Chianti, Tuscany and was established as a military/administrative hilltop fortress. The village is widely believed to be the birthplace of Amerigo Vespucci, one of Italy's greatest explorers and financiers. Until a century ago, most of the cottages in the walled village were linked by underground tunnels, so occupants could travel undetected between houses in case of attack. Montefioralle was in fact attacked in 1325, by Castruccio Castracani, with sections of it destroyed. These, along with the Church of Santo Stefano, were rebuilt over the following century.

Sitting at 500 metres above sea level, Montefioralle is cooler than Florence and Greve in summer and of course colder in winter, often surrounded by snow during the coldest months. The climate also ensures a unique blend of dry, cool summer months in which the grapes will ripen. The relative coolness allows these Chiantis to ripen more slowly than their cousins lower down, thus producing wines of greater finesse and structure, lower alcohol levels and a much longer cellaring life. I am no expert on olives, but I assume that the olives grown here at this altitude would benefit in similar ways. We certainly notice the difference in temperature and humidity on our daily walks down to Greve and back. During our stay the climate is perfection itself - endless sun, with a cool, dry breeze. The nights, even in April, are cold and perfect for sitting by the fire with a glass or two of elegant Chianti.

There are no vehicles allowed into the village, so it remains quiet and undisturbed. In fact, the serenity is palpable. At night the silence becomes like *white noise*. After the birds have ceased their song for the day and the villagers fasten themselves into their stone cottages for the night a blanket of mute stillness descends over the village. There is no traffic, no exhaust fumes, or horns, or screeching brakes, nothing except the absolute silence that comes with such a seemingly remote place. Sleep comes quickly and deeply until we are woken each morning with a chorus of birdsong. It seems too idyllic to be true, but here the gentle passage of time is full of natural wonder.

Our apartment

Let me indulge and take a moment here to describe our apartment, because I really did fall in love the moment I saw it. It's set on the western edge of the hill, embedded in the protective wall surrounding the entire village. You turn in and down from the village's single street that runs in 360 degrees. The apartment itself has eighteen-inch-thick stone walls that provide incredible insulation in summer but unless you have the heaters on in winter, can turn the place into an ice-box. On entering the apartment, you move from the ancient to the modern in the space of a doorstep. Colours are typically Tuscan, with lots of burnt orange, browns and blues, tiled floors and rendered white walls. Stepping outside the apartment, you have the wonderful turfed terrace that looks out to the west and down across the sweeping vineyards and olive groves that surround Montefioralle on all sides. The views stretch for many miles in a 180-degree arc, providing us with a panoramic backdrop. We soak these views in day after day and dream of never leaving.

Farmers throughout Chianti traditionally nurture and harvest both grapes and olives. The region's slopes are steep providing a cascade of peaky hills and declivitous valleys, one after another. Vineyards are perched precariously on the most dramatically abrupt hills with groves of olive trees bordering them. I can only imagine the difficulty in farming such a land of extreme gradients. Yet we watch exactly that happening. It is pruning season for olive trees and each farm has several men on ladders in trees, hand pruning the many branches. It is a long and onerous task, as most farms have several hundred trees which are laboriously pruned by hand. The off-cuts are gathered into piles and set alight, with small smoke spirals rising across each hill. As we walk past these small groups of men, they stop their work and call out a cheery 'Bonjourno' with a generous smile. We return the greetings and attempt some small talk, asking about their trees and how previous weather conditions have helped or hindered their bounty.

This most native of Italian practices is suffused with tradition. Olive harvesting in much of Italy has been going on for the past four thousand years and a number of the olive varieties cannot be found anywhere else in the world. Most of the trees themselves are between 150 and 400 years old with organic practices dating back to the 1400s. You can imagine the soil quality after 600 years of organic treatment and care. Italian households consume roughly 1,000 tonnes of organic olive oil per year, a small percentage of overall oil consumption. Thus, the Chianti region ranks as one of Italy's most prestigious olive oil producers, where yields are smaller per hectare, but quality is extremely high. As with wine, geographical and quality designation is rigid, so that to acquire a Tuscan or Chianti Olive oil label, farmers must meet strict criteria that ensure quality and low acid levels are maintained.

In vineyards here the soil is largely a white rubble of chalk and limestone – exactly the type grapevines love. In fact, *most* of the soil here is chalky white. The vines are just beginning to shoot, so in the past week vineyards have turned from brownish to deep green. They are meticulously spaced with perfect canopy management. These vines are all dry grown and from appearances, are organic in nature, as dictated by the DOCG. These are the characteristics that make Chianti wine famous the world over, wine, that like the region, is authentic, natural, and a true representation of its soil. Like their neighbouring olives, grape yields are low in these vineyards, which further improves the taste and quality.

****

There is an *earthiness* here that you don't find in many places today. These people somehow seem closer to nature, more genuine in their approach to life. Many of them are farmers and so are in touch with the soil, with the weather. They rise early and don't tend to stay up late at night. They are interested in the very tangible elements of daily life, looking after their crops and stock, ensuring that there is good food on the table, that their basic needs are looked after and that there is adequate preparation for the next season and harvest. You can't help but be infected by this "realness". There don't seem to be the usual sanitised or materialistic hang-ups that plague many Western societies. What you see here is precisely what you get, without the trimmings, without the melodrama, and without false expectations.

When you buy fruit or vegetables, instead of the washed clean and sterile presentation you get at home, here it comes complete with stalks and a coating of soil, as if picked and plopped straight onto the shelves. There is no apology for the presentation. This is local produce that has come straight from the farm to you without the attendant decoration or special packaging. And it speaks for itself.

The market town of Greve

Each day, regardless of whatever else is happening, we find ourselves making the trek down to the township of Greve. Backpacks are a permanent attachment, to be filled at the local co-op and butchers with our ingredients for the evening meal along with the mandatory bottle of Chianti. Then it's the trek back uphill, usually with an overflowing gelato in hand. We figure the exercise more than compensates for the calories... hopefully. But the main reason for shopping each day is because we can't resist the food. It is fresh and ripe and locally produced. We buy cheeses, cold meats, beautiful fruit and vegetables, breads all locally sourced and seemingly picked or delivered in the last 24 hours. It's usually organic and only slightly more expensive than the mass-produced stuff. Everything is just so cheap and fresh, and an €8 Chianti caps it off nicely. The idea of drinking *Chianti* in *Chianti* never loses its appeal.

On Saturday morning the central piazza in Greve hosts its weekly produce and wares market. This is a major event for the township and surrounding villages. Heading down at 10.am, the square is already overflowing with stalls of all kinds and crowds of locals. There are stalls selling leather goods, as there are everywhere in Tuscany. They are also selling fruit, vegetables, cold meats, cheeses, linen, shoes, clothing, and gelatos. Customers are loudly haggling over prices and pointing animatedly at the items they want. Each stall counter is deep in customers as they jostle for the most appealing items. Small groups of elderly locals gather in corners of the piazza laughing and talking, telling jokes and obviously enjoying their weekly catch-up with neighbours and friends. It's wonderful to wander through this scene observing local life, participating in a slower, simpler community tradition.

We use Greve as our central orientation point from which to walk and sight-see. Most of the villages in the area spread out in a rough circular pattern from the town so it is quite easy to navigate. It's actually an amateur historian's paradise in this region, because, as one of the oldest and most noble regions in Italy, Chianti is home to numerous abandoned, as well as inhabited, fully functioning castelló that date back to the Middles Ages. No matter which track, or "white road" you take around these hills you will come across at least one, if not more castelló (castles) or grand villas. They range from modest to grand and from derelict to beautiful, well-maintained estates, complete with residence, acres of parkland, the attendant olive grove or vineyard and a swathe of domestic help. Castello di Meleto, Castello di Speltenna, Castello Vicciomaggio, Castello di Querceto, and Castello di Brolio are just a few that dot these hills. They can usually be seen from some miles off, dominating their landscape and providing key reference points along the walking trails. Each one has its own long, well-recorded and often dramatic history, with links to the Medicis, Strozzi, Corsini, Frescobaldi, Machiavelli, Vespucci and other leading aristocratic families that shaped much of the medieval history in this area.

Day Trip to Firenze

This trip, we are only in Florence very briefly. One day to be precise, so I won't even attempt a full description of sights and feelings. Rather, a synopsis of the city and its history will have to suffice.

There is an early morning bus from Greve to Florence and we need to be on it. Today will be spent in Tuscany's largest city, for a day of shopping, sight-seeing and a little history thrown in. The cost of today's bus ticket is markedly different from the original trip here, even though the route is identical. It is not so surprising, as each time we catch the bus between common destinations in Tuscany, the prices change for no apparent reason. In fact, I suspect the bus driver just makes it up on the spot. Each time we state our intended destination, he looks at us, thinks for a bit, then seemingly pulls a figure out of the air. Quite typical of the way Italians do things, a bit randomly, with scant regard for regulations, and at the apparent whim of whoever is in charge.

After hurtling along the same narrow, winding roads with no thought for oncoming traffic, our driver delivers us into the heart of a congested, busy Florence. For a city of only 400,000 people the traffic comes as a shock. So does the pollution. Thick brown haze hangs in the air, smudging the distant landscape and the numerous church steeples. It is obvious where it comes from. Thousands of cars form a continuous arterial flow through every street in the city. Horns are blasting, drivers hanging out of windows yelling at or to each other, five or six rows of cars attempting to get into two lanes of roadway simultaneously. We approach the first pedestrian crossing and again, no-one takes the slightest notice. It is clear the cars have no intention of stopping or even slowing down so we just run between them and the speeding mopeds until stepping into safety on the opposite sidewalk.

Florence is located a mere 140 miles or so from Rome and is the capital of the province of Firenze and the region of Tuscany. It is even today, surrounded by the Tuscan hills in which large, palatial villas nestle with views over their olive groves and vineyards. The city dates back to about 900BC when settlements developed along the Arno River. Around 650 BC the Etruscans moved in and stayed, developing farmland and vineyards until the mid-1st century BC, when the Romans rose to glory, settling the region as a military base within their burgeoning empire. Ports were built at both Arno and Mugnone, from where military supplies could be transported and later, expanding trade. The continued development and expansion of the area guaranteed that the city would develop rapidly as a commercial and business base, quickly becoming one of the wealthier centres of the empire. And that takes us up to the late-Medieval period when the city underwent a rapid transformation of culture, commerce and politics.

Florence became the cradle, or crucible of the Renaissance. It could well be argued that this single city and its inhabitants gave rise to modern thought, to our current understanding of and appreciation for the great works of literature, architecture, sculpture, design, most forms of high art and even science. No other city can lay claim to so much progress in so many fields as Florence. For that, we owe a great and enduring debt. It is also home of the great Medicis, the family who can most of all claim responsibility for the Renaissance and who remained its custodians throughout several centuries. Through sponsorship of figures such as Leonardo de Vinci, Michelangelo, Donatello, Raphael and Galileo the Medicis ensured that the Renaissance would not only survive but continue to thrive, leading the world into a new and unparalleled knowledge of the Arts and Humanities. But the family was also the world's first true global bankers and modern businessmen. It came to command the rise and fall of governments, the flow or retraction of capital and even whether a country would go to war or not.

The Medicis first came to notice in 1230. By the early 1400s it was already a name associated with influence as Cosimo, the elder of the family, rose to prominence through his banking and political activities. Cosimo received much of his financial training in the Council of Constance before in the 1460s, moving on to manage the Vatican's finances, a development which underpinned the family's next iteration into extreme wealth and power. Through strategic loans to Kings, Lords, numerous aristocrats and national leaders, the Medicis built an empire of unrivalled influence that ensured wealth would continue to accumulate in the family coffers for centuries to come.

Fourteenth and fifteenth century Florence was a Medici stronghold and their reign over the city as well as their instalment of four popes placed them securely in the 'untouchable' class. If you climb the many steps to the platforms high above the city you can still see Medici Villas and the Belvedere Fort that was built for their protection with an array of impenetrable walls and underground tunnels. In the main square there are the fabulous Palazzo Pitti from where the family commanded its city, and the Ponte Vecchio, a covered bridge that was constructed to link the Palazzo Vecchio with a newer Medici palace across the river. It was constructed on top of an existing bridge but was separated and sealed from the 'commoners' so the Medici family could pass from one palace to the other without being seen or more importantly, attacked by jealous rivals.

Under the family Florence eventually emerged as a major rival of Rome. In later years the Papacy struggled and often failed to maintain influence over this city and came to see the family as an increasingly ominous threat to its own power base. But for most of their reign the Medicis were simply too wealthy and powerful for any effective suppression by Rome, leading to an uncomfortable truce that lasted on an off for many years between the two cities.

Florence still has many remnants of that earlier wealth and privilege. It still houses great names of fashion and sophistication, names such as Gucci, Hermes, Prada, Mont Blanc, Tiffany's, and numerous others that shine under Florence's legacy. But today, Florence no longer hosts a ruling aristocracy, and in some ways has fallen under Rome's shadow. Much of the privilege and wealth has eroded or been diffused and the great Medici family has fallen, with only scattered heirs to represent its name, but no longer its wealth.

But the city remains a host of world-renowned attractions such as the Uffizi Gallery, where some of Italy's greatest artwork is housed. Here hang masterpieces by Da Vinci, Giotto, Michelangelo and Botticelli, masterpieces that still capture our imagination and provide a glimpse into the genius of the middle-ages and the early renaissance. There is the Academia Gallery where you can view Michelangelo's "David", or the magnificent Duomo, which includes Giotto's Bell Tower, as well as the Opera Museum and the grand Cathedral. Such attractions will inspire the most sceptical among us, providing a unique insight into the grandeur and creative brilliance that defined medieval Florence.

The other version of the city is of course, its tourism hub. No matter which direction you take, there are markets, restaurants, boutiques, fashion houses, artisans and jewellers, all plying their trade to the thousands of cashed-up visitors who crowd these streets on a daily basis. The city reminds me of a frantic beehive, a bustling epicentre of activity that only slows with sundown, sighing, recovering and renewing before the next day's onslaught.

Florence, however, is more than these characteristics. It is above all, the beauty, spectacle, vibrancy and enrichment of a living, interactive museum, one that doesn't just display but injects energy and wonder into each of its visitors. It is a city that remains uniquely bewitching and captivating, a city that despite all its flaws will leave a visitor craving more, vowing to return, never quite sated with

its charm. In many ways, Florence is the essence of all that Italy represents, its dreams, its sorrows, its mistakes and its far-reaching achievements.
****

The bus home was much the same as the ride in, except of course the fare was different again. At a village still 10kms north of our own, the driver brakes and pulls the bus over to the side. With no warning, front and rear doors open and the driver steps out onto the side of the road to light up a cigarette. While Wendy and I look on, half the passengers get up and follow him. For the next ten minutes they stand around, smoking, and chatting. Wendy and I sit slightly dumbfounded at what appears to be a normal ritual. Then with a grunt from the driver, they all pile back on and we continue our journey. Finally, we are happily back in our beloved Montefioralle, cooking pasta, drinking our favourite Chianti and planning the days ahead.

Walking through Chianti

Our host had advised us when we arrived that we should hire a car because there really was nowhere to walk in the area. This was quite depressing, because walking was one of our reasons for coming here. We had wanted to spend a good amount of time just relaxing and taking long, quiet walks in the Chianti hills. Fortunately, our host had very different ideas about what represented walking. When looking for trails on the Internet next morning we find recommendations for a whole array of Strada Bianche or *white road* routes passing by our village and into the hills for miles beyond. The map is literally criss-crossed with trails. Looking out from our terrace we can actually see half a dozen of these *white roads* leading off in different directions from a junction just below us. In fact, we learn soon enough that Italians are not particularly big on walking. They try to avoid walking unless it's to cover a very short distance with minimal effort involved. Why walk when they can hop on their beloved mopeds and zoom from one neighbour's house to the next, all within a 500-metre range. And yes, there are many, many steep hills around Chianti, and you *do* need a certain level of fitness to attempt them. But the scenery from these walking tracks is so spectacular that the climb is worth it. You really do see so much more of an area when you walk rather through it. I find driving rather an insular mode of transport. You are moving along a strip of tar at speed, inside a metal and glass bubble that seals you off from the world, from all sound, from fresh air, from myriad different scents. Scenery flashes past providing only the merest glimpse of the environment through which you are moving. There is no experience. There is no participation. You are little more than a casual observer for the briefest time. How on earth can you get a 'feel for a place' inside a car.

I think the best decision we made was to *not* have a car for our time in Chianti. This allowed us to experience the environment at its best, to participate in an unhurried, deliberate way, to soak it up and extract the real essence of this secluded oasis. Walking along dirt trails, crunching the white chalk beneath you, smelling the sweet, olive-scented breeze, or seeing new Spring leaf-growth on grape vines, is a completely delightful involvement that only walking can give. You feel the changes in air temperatures and currents. You hear the comforting noises of village life as you approach the little groupings of houses. You hear the constant, gentle birdsong that filters through these days from sunrise until well after dark at night. You feel the ebb and flow of Chianti life.

Our first big walk was to the neighbouring village of Panzano. This turned out to be approximately four hours with the first two thirds of the walk being continuously, steeply uphill. We simply kept climbing, often thinking that we had reached the top only to see the track plateau slightly before climbing again. By the time our destination was finally reached we were hot, sweating and tired. The days in Chianti have been warmer than usual for this time of year, often four or five degrees above average. While we stood at the top fanning ourselves and taking large gulps from our water bottles, an Italian woman, with a serious looking face, passed us on what we guessed was her daily run. Despite the warmth of the day, she was wearing thick black tracksuit bottoms, a long-sleeved top, with a padded short-sleeved coat over that. Her face was bright red and she grunted a quick "Bonjourno" before sucking in more air. A little over an hour later, the same woman passed us again on her way back, still in her layers of clothing and now scarlet red in the face, sweat pouring from her, and with an even more serious facial expression. She looked ready to collapse.

What was beginning to dawn on me, and would continue to right through our Italian journey, was the way Italians soak up any heat and sun available, regardless of the season. Despite Rome and Chianti, and later the whole of Sicily, being quite a bit above the average temperature for this time of year, often in the mid-twenties Celsius, the locals continue to dress for a mid-winter climate. On a warm day you will see them sitting at outside cafes in the broad sun dressed in long pants, shirts, jumpers, and padded parkas. This is at the same time we are seeking shade and dressed in shorts and t-shirts. They simply don't appear to feel the heat.

Although the walk to Panzano is exhausting, the views are unsurpassed, with wonderful vistas in each direction. At one side there is a clear view right across Chianti to the distant city of Florence, with its brownish haze hanging over it. In other directions we can see distant castles, hillsides of grape vines, and tiny villages dotting the landscape. The walk takes you through endless vineyards and olive groves with local farmers out hand-pruning trees. They are sun-browned with black hair, creased, weathered faces and big, white teeth that flash as they smile. The fact that we are crossing their land uninvited is of no concern to them.

I guess everyone who travels has their own stories about which nationalities are friendly and which are rude or uninterested. Of course, these observations are usually generalisations because as in our own country, there are both lovely and not so lovely people scattered through every city and town. And yes, no matter what country you're in, people are generally friendlier in rural landscapes than their city counterparts. Life moves just that bit slower, giving more time for lost visitors and those of us who foolishly confine ourselves to a single language, usually not theirs. But I have to say, that regardless of where we are in Italy, whether it's the bustling, congested city of Rome, the intensely proud and autonomous island of Sicily, or among the rural affluent of Chianti, we never feel unwelcome or alone.

What really does become apparent as you walk these hills, is the amount of old wealth in the area. They are centres of substantial estates, acre after acre of vineyards creating some of Chianti's best wines. The residences are so large that each can be seen from miles off and will often cover an entire hilltop. Many appear to have an army of domestic workers - gardeners, cleaners, cooks, and housekeepers. A number are even beyond this scale, so vast that you cannot fit them into the camera lens, high security gates sealing them off from the world, acres of manicured gardens and guard dogs roaming the perimeter.

Recently, the Financial Times ran an article on sales of great estates in Tuscany, with billionaires now viewing the ownership of a famous Tuscan vineyard as a *must have*. In the past eight months, the Times claims, no less than four significant estates have changed hands for between €25 and €30 million. More commonly, smaller estates including a villa, 80 to 100 acres of vineyards, as well as olive groves sell for around €5 million, attracting plenty of buyers. But while a raft of new owners is entering the Chianti landscape, the old wealth of the area, the old families that have occupied this land for generations, still prevail. Many of its original families consider themselves at the pinnacle of Italian high culture, their province, more like an autonomous country, their family names sitting alongside the nobility in terms of heritage, culture and wealth.

After more exhausting hill climbs, we finally arrive in the medieval village of Panzano, a much larger village than ours and busier, but just as old. Panzano is exactly halfway between Florence and Sienna, and is, therefore, the perfect stop-off point for many tourists. This accounts for its *busyness* compared to our own village of Montefioralle. Also, it is the intersection of a number of important roads, as well as hosting several Chianti festivals each year. As with each of these villages, Panzano has its central church - the Pieve di San Leolino - located at the highest point of the village with commanding views over the surrounding villas and the land beyond. Panzano is geographically small with a number of local shops and bars, a central piazza and the pre-requisite ancient hill-top fort adjoining. In fact, in its day this village was the most fortified of all within the Tuscan region, due to it being home to the powerful Firidolfis, who reigned supreme for generations. Panzano's heyday occupies much of the twelfth century, when its leading families controlled significant chunks of Chianti. Its walled perimeter created an almost impenetrable defence, and its marketplace grew to be one of the most popular and heavily traded of all.

Cars *are* allowed into this village and the main road runs straight through the centre, weaving between houses and shops, climbing and dipping, so there is not the peace and tranquillity that we have become used to. Even trucks manage to squeeze themselves along these narrow lanes, making it less than pleasant walking along the main streets. But Panzano is beautiful nonetheless, perched so high up on the hill that its views stretch for miles in all directions.

After exploring the village on foot, we buy our obligatory gelatos and head to a local café while we wait for a bus to take us back down to Greve. The café owner and his son greet us warmly as we enter and find a seat. It's a tiny café but everything seems available – full meals, gelatos, milkshakes and even beer and wine - all served from the old narrow counter at the side. Liquor is available and consumed pretty well everywhere in Italy. Not only supermarkets, but cafes, delicatessens, grocers, even coffee shops and service stations throughout Italy sell copious amounts of liquor. You can buy beer, wine, whiskey, grappa, and by our standards, it is very cheap.

At the table next to us there are three old, Italian women, one of them almost bald. It seems that this cafe is their local haunt, by the way they converse with the owner, cracking jokes and pouring themselves coffee from the counter. They sit over their little short blacks passing gossip and smiling at us every couple of minutes. We feel included wherever we go. There is never hostility or wariness from the locals but instead smiling faces, acknowledging us and offering help whenever we seem in need. There is also surprise when we show up in walking gear, surprise that firstly, we are out walking, and secondly, that I am wearing shorts. When we tell our hostess where and for how long we walk, she looks at us with raised eyebrows and tut-tuts. The un-voiced question is always; why? And, either I have very strange legs or wearing shorts in Italy is some kind of unholy act. I, and other male tourists in shorts almost always attract bemused stares from the locals as we pass.

According to a recent article on Italian fashion, shorts apparently should be reserved for the beach. As a male in Italy, you are expected to wear casual business attire pretty well whenever you are not at work. More interestingly, it is also considered a fashion faux pas to wear shirts with any form of advertising on them. So, it seems my particular faux pas extends right across the dress code and unfortunately, I read this article late in our trip. To the fashion conscious Italians I must have caused deep offense.

We had numerous journeys on the "white roads" (*Strade Bianche*) of Chianti, leading us over its hills and into its valleys, through remote villages still turning their noses up at the modern world, past unending vineyards and olive groves, old fortresses, grand old *castelli* and large villas dripping with wealth. The White Roads are so named because of the white sand covering them and the chalk embedded in their sub-soils. They have been providing criss-crossing routes for Christian pilgrims and textile traders since at least the 10th century. In 2009 UNESCO declared this whole area a world heritage site, and it is easy to see why. Breathtaking scenery awaits every turn in the road and each village that punctuates these roads has its own historical significance, dating back centuries, marking famous battles, the downfall of an aristocratic family, or the birthplace of a cardinal.

A particular journey on one of these *white roads* leads us to the Badia a Passignano Abbey. The Abbey was constructed in AD 395 under the orders of the Archbishop of Florence, and is still home to several intransigent Vallombrosan monks today. The monks, who represented a reformed sect of the Benedictine tradition, produced a number of cardinals and even a pope. Their Pope rebuilt the ruined Abbey and helped entrench the Vallombrosan brand within the inner circles of the Catholic Church. The power and wealth of the Vallombrosans continued to grow through their influence in the church as well as vast landholdings accumulated throughout Tuscany. The monastery even played host to Galileo Galilei, from where he is known to have taught mathematics. In their day, the Abbey's monks specialised in wine making with grapes from their own vineyards, making some of the most renowned drops of the region. Even today, the Abbey has its own wine brand, still supplying local retail outlets and attracting awards for quality.

Our journey to the Abbey is a three-hour trek up long, steep hills with only short descents. It's a beautiful walk-through shaded wood, then along backbones of steep hills, with uninterrupted views of this magnificent Abbey from several miles off. The walk is difficult at times but always rewarding. It passes alongside a number of ancient stone estates that are still occupied by old Chianti families, tending their vines. The Abbey grows in size and magnificence as our approach nears. After taking a long, wooded lane to its doors, we stand at its front doors and take in the immensity of its walls and stone turret. The building looks impenetrable and I imagine, was designed that way to offer both real and symbolic protection to its cloistered residents. It is ringed by giant cypress trees and, like all abbeys in the region, sits atop one of the highest hills, signifying its physical proximity to God and removal from the heathen world below, but also commanding the surrounding landscape.

Upon arrival, there is a wait of more than an hour for the resident monk to rise from his siesta, chat with several of the villagers, be led into a little stone house by an extremely old and bent woman, and then, after some time, emerge to open the Abbey gates. But it was worth the wait to view the majesty and imperialism of such a medieval institution. The thick stone walls and high ceiling reduce temperatures inside by at least ten degrees. The interior is dark and musty and cavernous which lends a booming quality to our voices and creates echoes with each footfall. But the exquisite paintings and sculptures that line the walls, some close to a thousand years old, evoke enthralling images of the lives and events that this medieval symbol of religious authority has helped to shape.

A bucket on our heads

By 4.pm it is time to leave the village for the return trip if we're to make it home before dark. We emerge from the Abbey into a leaden afternoon. Once clear blue skies have become dark and menacing, with heavy, blue-black clouds sitting low on the hills. Quickly striding off up the road there is a fading hope that we'll make it home before the threatening downpour. And then hope fails completely. Less than a kilometre into our return journey the heavens let loose, perhaps on instruction from the Abbey, and the rain comes down in waterfalls. We huddle under a small, overhanging olive tree, providing scant protection, deciding that the only way of getting home without pneumonia is to hitch a ride.

After a further ten minutes of our waterlogged tree gradually lowering itself onto our heads, we hear the blessed approach of a car engine. A tiny, very old *Fiat 500* comes into view, with three large young men crowding its interior. I put my thumb out anyway. Surprisingly, it shudders to a halt with the back door swinging open. An arm extends followed by a toothy smile, beckoning us in. With much re-arranging of the interior, Wendy and I manage to squash ourselves into the cramped backseat beside one of the fellows and his building gear. Introductions are made with much smiling and waving of hands. We couldn't speak their language and they couldn't speak ours. From what we can determine, the three of them, a father and his two sons hail from Marrakesh. Apparently, their names are Mohammed, Mohammed, and *Gary*. Yes, that kind of stumps us too. How on earth do you get a *Gary* from Marrakesh? But the scary thing is that these introductions take place while we're travelling at high speed, in the rain, around tight bends on a very narrow road.

Making it immeasurably worse, is the fact that the driver keeps turning around to shake our hands over and over, smiling all the while. But still, he somehow manages to steer the car around these incredibly tight bends. Wendy has her eyes firmly shut for most of the journey, but after twenty minutes of this dangerously casual driving style we are miraculously delivered back to our tiny village of Montefioralle. Again, there are many grins and nodding of heads and, thanking them profusely we jump out, grateful to be back on firm land. They were exceptionally nice people. We learned along the way that they were actually heading in pretty well the opposite direction after they picked us up, but when we indicated we were staying at Montefioralle, with yet another smile and handshake they changed direction and took us all the way to our destination. It was at least 10 kilometres out of their way, a gesture of kindness that left a lasting impression.

Kindness and generosity continue to flow. Our host had recommended an authentic Chianti restaurant in Greve to us that offered each of its meals as either 'normal' or gluten free. This seems too good an opportunity to miss as I am one of those unfortunate beings that's been dogged by coeliac since birth. She had said it was a regular haunt of theirs and was well worth the walk down into Greve, so we head off next evening to try it out. The restaurant is rustic with a narrow entrance and cavernous interior. Three wait staff stand at the entrance. They bend low and offer us a most gracious welcome, ushering us inside. The son of the owner acts as maître de, another brother is headwaiter and the momma, who has owned this establishment for the past forty years, is in the kitchen cooking her traditional dishes. She comes out to meet us and it's obvious that she and her sons take great pride in their little establishment. She explains her dishes in detail, each description with a flourish of hands and head nodding by the sons. The restaurant has excellent reviews on Trip Adviser so we're quietly confident that we'll be enjoying the meal.

A few minutes later we are brought complimentary sparkling wine to have while we chose from an extensive menu. After reading through the offerings, all with ridiculously cheap prices and being assured that any meal we want can be prepared gluten free, we order an entrée and main, or *primi* and *secondi*. Our shared *primi* of polenta balls draped in roasted mushrooms and tomato sauce arrive with formal presentation. The dish is substantial and smells divine. It also turns out to be delicious! Every mouthful is a taste sensation. This woman has every right to be proud.

By the end of the *primi* we are already feeling fairly full, needing some time to let it settle and relieved that we had decided to share. But then our *secondi* arrive which are even larger. I had ordered a gluten free pizza, which quite simply, is one of the best dishes I've ever eaten. Despite the size of the meals, we manage to polish them off as well, washed down with some cheap but good Chianti. There probably isn't anything more authentically Italian than polenta, pizza and Chianti for an evening meal. We relax into our chairs, listen to the soft music and absorb the atmosphere of this delightful eatery.

When we finally ask for the cheque, we're told in no uncertain terms that we must wait. Slightly mystified, we indeed wait. Before long, complimentary dessert wines and actual desserts are brought to the table, also delicious. After we finish these, the cheque *does* eventually arrive. It could well have been just for the entrees, as it is far too low for what we have consumed tonight. Even after the mile-long climb back up the hill to our apartment, we are still feeling full, but truly satisfied, and again, with a feeling of genuine goodwill towards these wonderfully hospitable people.

Our next restaurant visit involves a beautiful and traditional eatery in Montefioralle itself. We had again read wonderful things about it on TripAdvisor and other restaurant sites that included rave comments about the chef's reputation. We had walked past this restaurant daily on our trips down to Greve and back and had salivated each time we approached it and were treated to the delicious smells wafting from the kitchen. It was more expensive than most in the area so the plan was to save our visit for the final night of our stay. The wonderful scents got the better of us, however, so we decided to make a booking for the next evening.

The restaurant had been in the family for four generations and, as we discover, is one of five restaurants owned by this extended family throughout Chianti. We enter the tiny wood-panelled room that accommodates maybe six tables and which is partitioned from the even smaller kitchen by a colourful red, green and white curtain. The waitress - the owner's daughter – is lively and friendly, laughing and swapping jokes with each of the guests. She keeps apologising to us for her poor English and we joke back that it's far better than our poor Italian. After chatting with her at the door for a few minutes, she ushers us to the table and provides menus. Momma is then led out of the kitchen to greet us. Wendy orders some Chianti, then a selection of starters and a main dish of wild boar, a dish neither of us has tried before. It is rich, meaty, and packed with a myriad of flavours. The boar has been slow cooking for many hours, falling apart on our forks as we try to restrain ourselves from hoovering it in. I didn't realise food could taste this good! After finishing the meal and more wine than we should have, and then squeezing in a sumptuous desert, we ask for the cheque. The waitress replies; "No first you must have some of our Grappa and Limoncello on the house". Really? What is with the complimentary drinks and how do these people ever make money?

So, after two bottles of wine, we embark on some very potent but delicious cypress grappa, then strawberry grappa, followed by shots of Limoncello. The waitress hadn't supplied these liquors in the usual small glasses, but instead, had placed four large bottles in front of us with the instruction to have as much as we want. We followed her instructions. The alcohol level of these drinks is much higher than your average wine, so suffice to say that we are somewhat the worse for wear leaving the restaurant and slurring our goodbyes. We stumble back to our apartment, the distance seeming a lot further in reverse. I'm pretty sure we do one circuit too many of the village before finally locating our lodgings. But what a night! We felt welcomed, included, pampered, happy, and totally contented. These people have a way of making you feel good about pretty well anything. Without appearing to try they provide you with evocative and memorable experiences. I think it's because their own love of life, of food, of wine, of company is so infectious. Life in these villages, among these people, can be distilled into the simplest but most profound pleasure. Simplicity has a way of cutting through the *noise* of life, the things that detract and distract. It has the capacity to deliver a purer, unadulterated version of what it is that you crave. Here, in Montefioralle, simplicity is a way of life.

Next day we are invited to our host's vineyard for some wine tasting. There is still a tendency to associate Chianti wine with the *fiasco-style* squat bottle wrapped in a straw blanket. But such perceptions are more tradition than actual. Yes, they still sell those squat bottles but mainly for tourist purposes. Chianti wines today are rather more sophisticated, ranking with some of the best in the world and earning a large chunk of the country's wine revenue. Jancis Robinson, one of the world's most renowned wine critics, has referred to Chianti as Italy's Bordeaux due to its excellent blending of grape variety and its growing reputation for quality.

The winery visit is framed by a gorgeous day of blue skies and cool breeze, as almost every day has been so far. We sit up high on the winery's balcony drinking in the view while also drinking the full range of the host's wine offerings. Surprisingly, this range, unlike most other Chiantis, tastes quite *Australian*, a bit heavier and fruit-driven than most. But the winery is relatively young and its product will probably develop with age. The afternoon here is spent consuming cheese, biscuits and bruschetta and rather too much vino. As the sun begins to ride low in the sky and a cool breeze picks up, we reluctantly leave our panoramic perch to amble back down into Greve. Quickly grabbing some ingredients for dinner at the local Co-op, we trek back up the steep hill to our homely apartment. Needless to say, we sleep early and well that night but rise with a sore head next morning.

Despite our vows of abstinence, or at least a reduction in liquor, before beginning this trip, the opposite is in fact happening. At the start of each day, we vow a day of minimal cheese, chips and wine. By the end of each day, our vow has disintegrated to the point that again, too much cheese, too many chips, and too much wine is consumed. It is just so relaxing here that you feel you must do it justice by indulging in all your sinful pursuits. I mean, just picture this: late afternoon arrives, the sun is low over hills spread with olive trees and vineyards, we have a beautiful terrace that looks out over all this and it is time to wind down for the day. Is there any better way to enjoy an oncoming sunset than with cheese, chips, and olives all washed down with yet another superb Chianti? If that isn't the most fitting way to end your day then please, tell me what is? At least walking to exhaustion most days, helps slow the expansion of our waistlines.

On one of our final days in this exquisite place, we take the long uphill trek to Castella di Uzzano. This castle, now in private ownership, once belonged to a self-made and self-styled aristocrat – Niccolo da Uzzan. During the mid-1500s he rose to great prominence in the region and believed firmly in his equal status to the Medicis, a belief that was not, unfortunately, shared by others. His obsession with the famous family and his incessant need to challenge their dominance became so consuming that he took it upon himself to scheme their downfall. He of course failed dismally. Their dominance and wealth continued to swell and Uzzan retired a broken man to his castle in Chianti to live out his days in bitterness.

In its present form, the Castle remains an imposing estate. Like all castles in the area, it is perched high upon a hilltop with commanding, 360-degree views. It is secluded, with giant fir trees encircling its prodigious and beautifully manicured grounds. The estate, also like so many other grand estates in Chianti, has its own wine brand, although the vineyards from which these are produced are separately owned. These estates require a substantial fortune to maintain their buildings, grounds and staff so although the current owner remains anonymous, the funds at his/her disposal must indeed be significant.

Afternoon delight

I discover that each afternoon around 2 or 3.pm, the small tree-lined piazza in the centre of Montefioralle becomes the meeting place for three of the village's elderly women. There are four benches in the piazza but the women always choose the same one, facing the village church. They sit in the same formation each day, the two older women on the outside with the younger of them in the centre. She knits intently and rarely lifts her head from her work. The two older women both have walking sticks, which they lean on while they sit. They stare straight ahead while making occasional remarks to each other. The younger one sits and nods at each comment without lifting her eyes from her knitting.

I undertake to turn up in the piazza at various times in the afternoon to watch them for a small stretch as inconspicuously as possible. They usually stay for two to three hours depending on the weather, this daily ritual probably extending over years. The two older women are approximately eighty years of age while the younger is perhaps in her mid-sixties. She may be a daughter or niece of one or maybe just a friend, but the relationships seem close. There is rarely any change to their routine and I wonder if they do this all year, even in winter. I would love to eavesdrop on their conversation. Possibly they talk of the tourists visiting the village, but more likely they indulge in some village gossip and discuss the state of the olive or grape harvests. It is a ritual that marks the slow rhythm of this secluded little village. It is one of the symbols I love so much about this place.

On our walk down the cobbled lane to our apartment we must pass the village bar. This is not your usual bar. It opens most afternoons for three hours or so but there are no set days. Then it might open again in the evening, if the patron feels like it. When talking to the woman herself about her opening times she replies: "Sometimes I open, sometimes not". No further explanation is forthcoming. You just have to hope that if you feel like a beer or wine, then her feelings correspond with yours. The inside of the bar is incongruous. At first glance it looks like an American milk bar. There are plastic tables and chairs, lots of bright colours, a tiled floor and a plastic bench from which the barmaid serves. The room is actually an extension of the woman's house. It feels very strange drinking alcohol in such an environment. There is no indication that it's a licenced establishment.

Perhaps it's not. I think it more likely that the landlady just decided to open up her sunroom and start serving liquor. I like the fact that these people just to do their own thing, if they feel like it, when they feel like it. I like their contempt for the requirements and punctuality and standardisation that modern life attempts to impose. I like the way they conduct their lives according to emotional needs rather than analytical ones. They suit themselves and behave as the will takes them.

Moving on

Unfortunately, it is now time to leave our beloved Chianti. We are both feeling rather despondent and reluctant to say our goodbyes. Tomorrow we head off to Palermo, Sicily, but for now, I sit and think over our experience here, indulging in the soft glow of a special time. It has elicited feelings that I have rarely felt, experiences that stir deep emotions. Chianti has imparted warmth, a generosity of spirit, a beauty and grace, and most of all, a rhythm of serenity that leaves you feeling fulfilled and content. My spirit found solace in the hills and ancient villages of this area. It felt renewal. I leave this beautiful land feeling lighter, reinvigorated. I know that I will return.

Chapter Three: Smoke and Mirrors in Palermo

Arrival in Palermo comes after a long day of travel. Palermo is Sicily's capital and largest city. We have been on the go since 8.am this morning, first, on a local bus from Greve to Florence, then on an intercity bus to Florence's rather small and insignificant airport. Here we boarded a flight to Rome, where there was a two-hour layover, before taking another flight on to Palermo. It is now 3.pm and there is still another one-hour shuttle ride into the city of Palermo where our apartment hopefully awaits. But first there is the job of extricating ourselves from Palermo's airport, which is proving somewhat more difficult than we expected. After disembarking from a smallish passenger jet out on the runway, where it has been sitting for the last thirty minutes, we board one of the crowded runway buses that deliver us to the baggage claim area. Here, we wait .... and wait. After forty minutes our baggage belt, with a clank and an unhealthy groan, finally starts moving. With considerable relief we shuffle up to collect our bags.

Far too pre-emptive. One lone bag is ejected onto the belt. After many more minutes another two come on. We wait for what must be ten minutes before, with some excitement, we see a whole bunch of bags come on one after another. Everyone shuffles further forward and begins jostling for a better position. A few lucky travellers collect their bags and smile self-righteously at the rest of us. Then the belt stops. Another wait. Nothing. People begin checking the board again, wondering if the bags have been diverted to a different belt. After another eternity several of us wander over to the "Complaints Desk" to find a very relaxed official who smiles knowingly at us and tells us not to worry. "Your bags will come. You must be patient". So, we wander back and after more waiting the conveyor belt cranks back into action. The single bag ritual starts up and one by agonising one, they come down the line.

A full two hours after entering the baggage claim area, we are finally leaving. The next stage of torture involves the shuttle trip to our apartment along roads where the speed limit reads 100kms, but our driver sits on 160kms. He doesn't speak English and our Italian is rubbish, so we just cling to the door-handles in silence and await our fate. At this speed we arrive much sooner than anticipated, emerging from a dirty van into an even dirtier street. The coastal drive to the city was quite beautiful, with rugged hills and mountains on one side, and an incredibly blue ocean on the other. But here, in the middle of the city, beauty is harder to find. Our host is waiting for us outside the apartment complex and leads us up five long flights of stairs, through building construction on all sides (which the website failed to mention) and at last into our apartment.

The place is attractive and well appointed, with the exception of the balcony, which was the main drawcard for us, facing directly onto the construction works about three metres away. The noise is deafening (another issue they failed to mention). When mentioning the long delay at the airport to our host, she simply smiles and says "It's Sicily. People take their time here. They were probably having coffee." "Yes, but it was two hours" we reply. "That's right", she says, "No-one hurries here. They do things in their own time". We looked out at the construction workers in dismay. I imagined that they would also take their time.

Palermo is a city that takes some getting used to. I have to say that so far, Wendy likes the city, but I think I will take more convincing. Again, like other Italian cities, it is chaotic, mainly because of the traffic and a blatant disregard for road rules. They seem to make a bit of a game of it, always with three or four traffic lanes attempting to get into one. But they are not even trying to go in the same direction. Cars are doing U-turns in the middle of three lanes of traffic, they are coming in at right angles from side streets and nudging into bumper-to-bumper traffic. They ignore red lights and pedestrian crossings. People cross anywhere on the street. Cars stop in the middle of rush hour so their drivers can jump out to talk to someone they recognise, or to duck into a nearby shop. There is a casual approach that sticks its finger up at any expectation of order. You could spend hours just watching the charades of city driving.

Wandering through the sprawling, congested, but often entrancing city, we wonder at the puzzling displays of overt wealth mixed with abject poverty. There appears to be little delineation, no real socio-economic boundaries between them. The main street has its Pradas and Guccis, Monte Blancs, Zegnas and more, with black Mercedes limousines cruising conspicuously between each. But a single block away, along the so-called beach-front, where you would normally expect the more expensive real estate, you are confronted with the depressing underbelly of a city that for too long has been neglected by too many.

Houses along the seashore are every bit as neglected as the public parks, the galleries and theatres, the street facades. Their paint is peeling, empty bottles and plastic rubbish decorate their lawns and bed sheets hang as curtains in cracked or broken windows. Yet strolling past them are couples dressed in immaculate, expensive suits on their way to somewhere less depressing or emerging from Audis and BMWs to enter a high-end Italian fashion house on the opposite side of the road. There are three distinct levels of government operating in Palermo - the Communal, the Provincial, and the Regional – but perhaps the number of government agencies stifles real attempts at social and economic reform.

To a casual observer, Palermo is a forgotten city, a city of disenchantment and poverty, where "survival of the fittest" reigns supreme. Perhaps the most symbolic marker of this poverty is the city's Botanic Garden. The cost to enter is five euros each, the only Botanic Garden I have ever paid to get into. It is a garden of sad decay. Obviously, the entry fee is to compensate for the city's financial inability or reluctance to sustain a place of pride and beauty. Pathways are crumbling, plants are dying, statues have been vandalised and the lawns are a depressing shade of brown through lack of care. Many of the plants are in broken pots and have not seen water for several weeks. The displays are uninspiring. We walk through the entire garden without spotting a single gardener or maintenance person. The only employee appears to be the man selling tickets, and he is most likely a volunteer.

We leave feeling rather downhearted. A walk along the beach promenade is similarly disheartening. After battling the madness of Palermo's traffic to get there, we are forced to walk along a congested highway for more than a kilometre because the beachfront has, for some obscure reason, been fenced off with rusting barbed wire. When a pathway to the promenade is finally found through discarded paint tins and household garbage the long, pebbly beach is deserted. There are one or two little carts with men selling gelatos but no customers to make their day worthwhile. It reminds me of Blackpool on a bad day, and that's saying something.

Sitting on one of the concrete benches we are approached by an African immigrant (of which there are many in the underclass of Palermo) of about thirty, who attempts to sell us leather wrist-bands and a pair of plastic sunglasses with pink lenses. We decline his offers but as usual, he won't leave. He keeps up the pestering, asking for two euros each. Finally, we get firm with him and eventually detach ourselves. But he is simply trying to scrape a living from a hard and unrelenting city.

Yet there is far more to Palermo that the casual observance. There is beauty woven intimately into the city's antiquity. Palermo was, after all, founded in the year 734BC, and its archaeological and historical wonders are indeed inspiring. First it was settled by the Phoenicians, the Sicans, Cretans and Elimi, then Carthage and the Roman Empire, before succumbing to the great Byzantine Empire, Arabs and eventually the Normans who saw it as one of the most attractive and sophisticated cities in Europe. Palermo still boasts the architectural influences of these many disparate realms. As one of the most invaded cities in Europe, its history is both richer and more eclectic than many as a result. The Palermo Cathedral, the Teatro Massimo, the Palazzo dei Normanni and the Capuchin Catacombs are testament to a city resplendent with endowments of the greatest kingdoms the world has known. In 2018 the city was named Cultural Capital of Italy, while in 2015 it was named European Capital of Street food and in 2016, gained World heritage status.

Wendy and I decide to visit one of the greatest of these endowments by setting off to the Palazzo di Normanni, or Norman Palace, which dates back to the 9th century and is recorded as the oldest royal palace in the whole of Europe. In the

11th century the Palace was further enlarged to become the Palace of the Norman King, Roger the 2nd and enjoyed an opulence that has evaded it ever since. True, it was restored in the 16th century, but its heyday of beauty and majesty was behind it. For the last few centuries, the Palace has acquired a different type of power as occupants have switched from royalty to politicians. Currently it is the headquarters of Sicily's Regional Government, which apparently finds it more satisfying to redirect funds that could be well spent on painting and patching the peeling facades, hallways, and exterior of the Palace, into their own internal Palace apartments where this opulence remains a central characteristic.

The centrepiece of the Palace is the Cappella Palatina – a magnificent chapel. Today it provides an insight into the splendour of early middle age religious symbols and the extravagant amounts of money expended in their construction. But like many other historical artefacts in Palermo, it now resembles a somewhat worn and slightly shabby facsimile of its former self. The funds for continual maintenance that are required for such masterpieces are sadly lacking and decay, therefore, has become an inevitable facet of its ageing. Nevertheless, the Palace provides a treasure trove of historical gems that will continue to provoke interest and pleasure for some generations yet. There are the most beautiful mosaics, paintings, sculptures and balconies. We spend hours appreciating this marvellous blend of cultural inheritance. It also serves to highlight the contrast of dark and light that *are* Palermo.

Another bright spot is the Teatro Massimo, Palermo's claim to the largest theatre in Italy and the third largest in Europe. And the Italians can rightfully take pride. It is simply spectacular, built in a traditional Greek/Roman style with ancient Sicilian additions and with all the architectural grandeur that such designs allow. Inside the Theatre visitors are treated to gorgeous claret-coloured marble columns interlaced with white swirls, elaborate drapes and ostentatious chandeliers over two stories of public foyer. The auditorium has five levels of public boxes as well as a large gallery. Throughout the Theatre, alongside rich fabrics are exquisite Murano glass exhibits.

If you move through to the Echo Room, as we were advised, you can take advantage of clever acoustics, which one imagines may have been devised for the purposes of somewhat dubious meetings or instructions. By standing in the absolute centre of the room, you can speak in a normal voice but your words will carry clearly to any other person in the room, even when crowded. If, however, you move to the edge of the room and again speak to your associate, you can even raise your voice and someone standing within a metre of your conversation will not hear a thing. It is a wonderfully eerie feeling.

The Theatre opened in 1897 with Giuseppe Verdi's production of Falstaff as its very first opera. Surprisingly, for the next forty years the Theatre was run by private enterprise, with different companies taking responsibility for each year's operas, usually a different company for each year. But after competition for production rights soured and funding issues replaced operas as the central consideration, the Italian Government took control and declared it a Public Theatre. Such a move, however, failed to relieve the funding crisis. In typical Palermo style, the lack of financial resources, combined with charges of corruption, political nepotism and a rapid escalation of debt continued to hound the reputation of the theatre, stifling efforts to initiate a renewed public funding model. This left an endowment of dilapidation.

While recently the arts schedule has been provided with a much-needed injection of morale and sponsorship through the appointment of a new director - Carapezza Guttuso - the actual structure has not been so lucky. Throughout the Theatre there are signs of deterioration almost anywhere you care to look. Much of the ceiling is in disrepair with large sections showing mould and whole sheets of paint peeling. And the attendant statues, sculptures and paintings have an uncared for, worn look, with accumulated dust, and chips/cracks in facades. There simply is not enough money or political will to bring the Theatre back to its former glory.

For me, however, this place is of particular interest. As an ardent "Godfather" fan it has special significance as the final location in the movie - Godfather 3 – in which Michael Corleone sat amongst the audience watching his daughter perform to great applause. As he left the Theatre in high spirits and looking forward to his future his daughter was gunned down, falling into his arms on the front steps in typical mafia fashion. It was indeed a moving scene and a notable moment in Al Pacino's acting career. The Theatre is also situated in one of the most attractive parts of the city, a large piazza – The Piazza Teatro Massimo Bellini - populated by numerous little restaurants and bars and at the end of a long, wide 'pedestrian-only' street. The street is lined with a mixture of authentic local and tourist-oriented shops with views to the surrounding hills, providing a dramatic background vista. This is a haven in an otherwise crowded and congested city. Here you can relax and take your time. You can take in the scenery, the cathedrals, the little boutiques, wonderful food markets and the street life that endows this area with a unique energy and vitality. I think if you spent your whole stay in this Piazza and its arterial street, you would fall in love. It is Palermo how it could be, and how it might be without its thick coating of corruption and black markets and diverted public funding.

The citizens of Palermo obviously see this area as a proud oasis too. With a double-take, Wendy and I spot a regional government worker leading a giant vacuum cleaner down the street. The vacuum is on very large wheels and the suction hose is about the size and shape of a rather large python. The whole contraption must have been six feet high and about four feet long, with the name "Glutton" printed along its side. The woman was actually vacuuming the street. It was obviously a common occurrence because no one else was taking the slightest bit of notice. Such an astonishing site demanded many photos and so I found myself following her along taking snapshots of this wondrous spectacle and the obvious pride she takes in her job.
****

It would be simple to make glib assertions about a city that can pack such a powerful punch and I must admit at first, I took a generally dim view of Sicily's capital. After some time acclimatising, however, you accept its deficiencies and learn to love its gritty, slightly shadowy atmosphere. You certainly admire and marvel at its history, much of its architecture and the unorthodox way it conducts it affairs. You can also be frustrated by the squalor that is often evident. You can despise the still flourishing black market, the crime, the substandard living of much of the population. You can be depressed by the apparent laziness of public bureaucrats, as well as the pervasive sewerage smell that dogs some quarters, the pollution, and the non-stop congestion.

But in the end, Palermo is an ancient city that has, over the centuries, millennia even, been influenced by the many civilisations that have invaded, conquered, colonised, and injected their own influences. The city and its people have learnt from, benefited and suffered under these influences. They have shaped the city's history and psyche and provided it with a complex fabric of daily life about which it is hard to make snap judgements. I suppose that's exactly what I meant at the beginning. You need time to get used to Palermo, to understand it and appreciate its contrasting characteristics. Only then, will you come to appreciate its enigmatic style, its gritty toughness, its refusal to bend to the will of governments and outsiders, its strangely seductive charm.

A Super Language

Something immediately apparent to any visitor to Italy is the ready and willing use of the English language. In Rome, Florence, Tuscany, and Milan you have little problem understanding or making yourself understood as an English speaker. Yes, there are exceptions and we have encountered a few, but they are just that, exceptions. Even in rural areas throughout mainland Italy and in much of Sicily, the English language is a common denominator when first languages fail to translate effectively. It is no real surprise, given that English has been a compulsory foreign language in Italian primary schools for the past fifteen years. Secondary and tertiary students continue their "English" education through specific mobility and communication programs that over the past decade have been gaining rapidly in popularity.

English, particularly in the larger Italian cities has become the "go to" language for commerce, socialising, and multi-ethnic interaction. At a restaurant in

Florence, for example, we observed with amusement a Russian gentleman, a German teenager and a Spanish woman making a number of attempts to converse about the food on offer. In frustration, the three finally resorted to English as the easiest way to communicate. Each of them grasped the English language enough to make themselves understood to the other, even with its inflections and inconsistencies. Add to that equation an Italian waiter who also conversed with the three of them in English and you understand the power and influences of this dominant *super language*.

Train stations, bus stops, airports, shops and public attractions have the Italian version with the English equivalent printed alongside or below. Italian radio has its talkback and advertisements in Italian but its songs almost exclusively in English. On Italian televisions you have a specific 'language' button to swap between Italian and English. You can watch many shows in either. The younger generation is fairly fluent in English. They can easily converse with you in either their native tongue or yours, whatever you choose. Embarrassingly, a number of business owners and public officials have apologised to us for their English not being 'up to standard'.

As an English-speaking person, you feel incredibly privileged and ignorant at the same time. The complacency is unsettling. We make no effort to understand their native language precisely because we don't need to. English is indeed the *super language* in the first instance because of its adoption and amalgamation over the centuries of Latin, German, Italian, Nordic, and French. It then blended, manipulated and simplified many of the adopted words and their derivatives to create possibly the most sophisticated language on earth.

In the second instance, the British Empire's global reach and colonisation between the 17th and 19th centuries ensured that this comprehensive language was spread across great and small countries alike and that its further adoption was adapted to become, if not a first language of a newly adoptive country, then at least a widely used second. Even those many countries hostile to the English and their culture, still, often against their wishes, absorbed much of the English language. It's adaptability, its sophistication, its wide usage of nouns and verbs, creates a universal appeal that is hard to ignore.

Today, English is the primary language of business across the globe, of trade, commerce, IT, and tourism, making it extremely difficult to escape its pervasiveness. As a result, the international community has shrunk, become more homogeneous than ever before and more able to communicate across borders and information channels. According to the renowned linguist David Crystal, "This is the first time we actually have a language spoken genuinely globally by every country in the world," More importantly today, English has increased its power and influence through Internet usage. It is estimated that over 80% of all Internet language is English. It is the language's cross-cultural elasticity that has really cemented its hegemony and which will protect it from future erosion. But again, I digress.

Chapter Four: Highway to Heaven

We are on the road from Palermo to Erice. I am happy to be moving on but have no idea what to expect from our next destination. Wendy has done all the planning and I have agreed without going into specifics myself or reading too much on each place. I am a tad lazy that way. But the excitement of the unknown is a journey in itself.

Our hired Fiat 500C is tiny. I feel that if we run out of fuel or get into a tight traffic spot, we could just about pick it up and carry it. The engine befits a car of this size so at 110kms it is screaming a high-pitched tone at us. But the car is new so it is handling the highway better than I had expected. Despite us sitting 10kms over the speed limit, cars are again flying past us at enormous speeds. Some are surely travelling in excess of 160kms as their slip-stream rocks our little egg on wheels. One after the other, they test the limits of their cars. Police cars also pass us traveling at the same speed. They're not in pursuit, just breaking the speed limit like everyone else. I don't really know why Italians bother putting speed signs up. They're redundant. Not only do cars pass us at ridiculous speeds, they do so in a relaxed, almost careless manner. As they flash past, they come close to brushing our little car, because it is obviously too much effort for them to change lanes completely. They remain half in our lane, half in the lane next to us. I guess this saves them moving *all* that way back into our lane after overtaking. Often, as we glance across at the overtaking driver, he or she is drinking coffee with one hand or talking on their mobile, even texting. Driving appears to be of secondary concern and I am mystified at the relative lack of road fatalities given their disregard for anything resembling safety. Italian drivers must feel a wonderful sense of freedom, driving as they wish, at whatever speed they wish with no real threat from authority.

In fact, the Italian Polizia have recently been issued with a fleet of custom-made Lamborghinis - the Italian supercar – capable of travelling at speeds in excess of 380kph and getting from a standing start to 100kph in under three seconds. From what I have heard while being here, the police test these figures regularly.

Once in a while you will see one of these Lamborghinis flash past, not pursuing anyone, just going really, really fast for the heck of it.

Perhaps on these highways at least, speed has something to do with the quality of the roads. Again, the high standard of Italian infrastructure surprises us, even in Sicily, where we expected everything to be starved of funds and in various degrees of decay. The roads are wide, safe and well built. Rather than saving money by going over or around hills as we do back home, Italians like to build tunnels, hundreds of them. Every major hill or mountain seems to be bored through with a tunnel, and every valley forded with a bridge, allowing roads to remain as straight and level as possible. Under optimum conditions, it is claimed that their tunnels can be bored at the mind-boggling rate of more than 22 metres a day. In fact, there appears to be little reluctance in spending billions to avoid these hills. For example, a relatively new highway connecting Bologna to Florence has no less than forty-five tunnels, viaducts and bridges to ensure that no hill or valley presents an obstacle. Mind you, the whole length of the road is only 65 kilometres. The machine that achieves this is a massive fifteen and a half metres in diameter and apparently is the most sophisticated 'dirt muncher' in the world.

The cost is estimated at approximately $9 billion. Where do Italians get this type of money, when they can't seem to stop their buildings from collapsing or pay for groundkeepers at their Botanic Gardens? Next, these highway-obsessed Italians are planning the world's longest and tallest suspension bridge between Calabria and Sicily. It is estimated that this will cost another $15 billion. If you are a bit of a tunnel or bridge spotter, then Italy is the place for you. But I have to admit that their dollars *do* make a difference. These roads are incredibly easy to drive on and hence, despite the recklessness of driving, it is probably harder to come to grief here compared to what we are used to in Australia.

In our tiny car we can't *flash* past anyone, so we have time to take in the amazing landscape through which we are driving. Also, Wendy doesn't usually last for more than thirty minutes or so without one of her eh, toilet stops. I have never known such a tiny or more insistent bladder. By now I am efficiently building these stops into our itinerary and journey times, which makes for much more organised travel.

Lush

I had always had visions of Sicily as a brownish land, partially desert or at least a sun-scorched landscape with not too much water, or anything else for that matter. I guess my ideas really came from the Godfather movie, with flashbacks to childhood in a land that was filmed in sepia, a nostalgic vision of relentless poverty and tough living. But as we drive across this larger than expected island we're confronted by a luxuriance of green foliage, of fruit trees, vines and prolific market gardens. It is rather startling in its vibrant relentlessness. It's a green that you would expect more in England than here in the hot climate of Italy's southern-most island.

There are thousands upon thousands of acres bearing olive trees, a variety of crops, vegetables, grapevines and most of all, citrus trees, with their colourful fruit hanging in luxurious abundance. It is far more agricultural than I had ever imagined. Little farm houses occasionally dot the landscape, swamped by their own crops, with citrus and olive trees as well as almond, walnut and hazelnut trees growing right up to the door in an attempt to extract as much food from the land as possible. Even more surprisingly, we learn that almost all crops in Sicily are organically grown. It's a land rich in the earth's produce. Many of these fruits and vegetables are sold locally through a myriad of Sicilian street markets that scatter themselves along the road network and populate many of the medieval alleys that wind their way through the island's towns and villages. The produce sits alongside market tables overflowing with freshly caught fish, locally produced cheeses, olive oil and a mind-numbing selection of salamis. The black market obviously remains alive and well, with no receipts, no tax and no records of what is bought or sold.

The contrasting colours of these field crops is beautiful. Deep greens clash with the yellow, orange and red fruits hanging low from their trees, along with carpets of blue and purple imprinted by acres of lavender, the gorgeous scent of which rushes though our open windows. It's a delight to the senses.

Most of the towns we pass through are small and compact, with apartments crowded together along hilltops or ridges. Apart from the farms, many people choose to live in close proximity, usually inhabiting blocks of three or four storey apartments along narrow streets before suddenly giving way to more farmland. The 'Aussie quarter-acre block' has no place in Italy. I imagine this practice of close hilltop living has its traditions reaching back through the centuries, when most towns or villages were compact and within stone walls for extra protection from invading foes. In fact, archaeological digs in a number of sites throughout Sicily and mainland Italy reveal remnants of circular stone walls not only around current towns and villages but most of the cities as well. People huddled together and sought out hilltops so that they might have additional warning of an approaching enemy. The practice has remained despite the threat no longer existing. While in centuries past this intense communal living also harboured and rapidly spread infectious diseases, including the Plague. Nowadays it mostly nurtures a sense of community, a connection with family, friends and neighbours upon which many of the more remote towns depend.

People spend a good deal of their after-work time outside, socialising with their neighbours and sharing the moments of the day over coffee or slightly more powerful concoctions. Often such gatherings last long into the evenings when food is brought out and shared in the local piazza and children play together while their parents exchange gossip. Unlike the Australian habit of shutting ourselves into our homes at night, away from all but our immediate families, these people see their brand of camaraderie as a vital ingredient to emotional nourishment.

As we leave Palermo further behind, the landscape changes from the rolling, sweeping hills of the past 150kms, to a flatter, more open landscape punctuated at regular intervals by steep and dramatic mountains. The farms, orchards, olive groves and vineyards take on a more severe appearance, clinging to steep slopes.

Even the soil looks more severe, with gravel and larger stones replacing the nutrient rich soil that was previously so common. The terrain tests our little car further, as its tiny engine tackles the challenging mountain roads, climbing and descending in monotonous repetition. Finally, after many miles of this mechanical torture, we find respite, as we enter a wide expanse of flat, unobtrusive, sameness. Ahead, in the distance, we see a dramatic mountain peak, with hints of an ancient village at the summit. We check our GPS and yes, this looks like it must be Erice – our next destination.

Chapter Five: A Rarefied Air

We were not at all prepared for what confronts us. Yes, the website told us it was a medieval hilltop village but this place stretches into the clouds. Its altitude is extreme and its isolation absolute. Our ascent begins, and the little Fiat is put into low gear for the formidable climb ahead. Ahead are six kilometres of the tightest switchback road I have encountered, doubling back on itself at each turn in an attempt to ease the gradient somewhat.

Suicide Street

Despite the best efforts of the switchbacks the road is so vertiginous that we spend most of the time in 1st gear with the engine struggling. Our adrenaline is encouraged further by the not so occasional cars coming down this treacherous road towards us. Apparently, day tourists drive up from the town of Trapani, located on the coastal plain far below. Unfortunately for us, they like to test their car's engineering by taking each corner as quickly and as widely as they can manage while keeping at least two of their wheels on the road. Wendy's usual habit of covering her eyes in such predicaments is a little chancy this time, as she happens to be the one driving. Several times she has to jump on the brakes to avoid a nasty bingle. Each time her face becomes a paler shade of grey and each time the oncoming car sails on past without slowing or even a glance in our direction. Her curses grow louder and less decorous.

Apart from the hellish drive, the scenery we are passing through is charming. Off to our right is a flock of extremely woolly sheep, each with a bell around its neck while a shepherd tends their needs. A melodic jingle rises from the flock as it moves across the hill, the shepherd and sheep dogs at a careful distance behind. I feel we've been transported back in time to a simpler, more rudimentary lifestyle. Small farmhouses can be spotted among several valleys leading away from the road. We see one farmer rigging his horse up to a manual plough, the type of which I know only through old photos from my grandparents' day. I am already feeling the seductive allure of this isolated outpost.

Eventually, we manage to change up into 2nd and then 3rd gear as the ascent gradually comes to an end. The vista that greets us is extraordinary. Wendy and I just stare in awe. We are actually above the clouds! I'm sure that with a powerful set of binoculars you see could the whole of Sicily from up here. This village is two and a half thousand feet above sea level, with views to Trapani, Marsala in the west, and the Aegadian Islands in the north-east. The day is clear with a cloudless blue sky. Cargo and cruise ships stretch out across the deep blue Mediterranean, tiny dots in its vastness. Even the town of Trapani below looks like a miniature Lego set from this altitude.The air up here feels thinner, lighter, and incredibly pure. It is also crystal clear. The walls surrounding this village were constructed by the Phoenicians in 750BCE, to guard their village and its ancient sites of worship. And it feels as if we have indeed entered a sacred citadel of the Gods.

Erice (first named Eryx) began as a Greek "polis", first mentioned by Thucydides as far back as 460BCE and the historian Herodotus in 425BCE. It is reputed to have been visited by no other than Hercules and Aeneas themselves. By all accounts, it was a centre of some importance, a large administrative centre, a formidable hilltop fort, and the regional exchange for currency (largely its own). Its wealth and influence continued to grow until the Carthaginians brought it to its knees in the first Punic War, a war from which it never fully recovered. Erice's influence waned and its importance as a commercial hub remained at best, secondary. But its archaeological legacy is a treasure trove for those seeking to understand the journey of civilisation.

By 250BCE, the Roman Empire had subjugated Erice, taking control of its fading commerce and injecting a military-style management into the community. Roman authority remained in place until the decline of the Empire, after which the next invaders - the Normans -established proprietorship in line with the rest of their Sicilian colonisation. Throughout the hilltop village's two and a half-thousand-year history and numerous invasions, however, Erice has successfully rejected all attempts to undermine its cultural integrity. Today, it is most renowned for its statue of Venus Erycina or, under the Greek mythological version, Aphrodite. Of course, over time myth succumbed to pleasurable trade and the legend surrounding this female God became a convenient euphemism for on-site prostitution. Not too surprisingly, this new 'entertainment' remained firmly in place regardless of which foreign power controlled the village.

Moving in

The fellow from whom we are renting our villa meets us in the car park. He is a large gentleman with an even larger smile. He is full of happy, energetic greetings, shaking our hands with vigour and continually clapping us on the back. We have read wonderful reviews about him and his place, so the anticipation is high. We pile into his battered minibus and he drives us to our apartment, weaving his way through unnaturally narrow lanes lined with tiny shops selling all manner of merchandise. Pretty well every panel on his car is dented and scraped and it quickly becomes obvious why. Often, the gap between our vehicle and the thick stone walls crowding every laneway is no more than a couple of inches. Sometimes it seems less. Each car we pass shares similar dents and scrapes and looks older than its years. It is one of the hazards of living here. You either walk or use a very old car. The lanes were obviously built for carts, not motor vehicles and the cobbles testify to their centuries of use with deep wheel ruts engraved into the worn stones.

The other quirk we notice, and one that will play havoc us during our stay, is that the village is completely circular, with walls so high that your view of surrounding streets is non-existent. Erice is by any standard old, and the stone apartments lining these streets testify to the centuries that have passed. Their permanency is their key feature, built of twenty-inch-thick stone that insulates and soundproofs and will most likely still be here in another thousand years. But there is a lean to them, their walls and eves running at strange angles, appearing to have no horizontal lines. Roofs dip and rise in random fashion. In fact, apart from the circular nature of the lanes, there is no architectural consistency here. I imagine living quarters have been built where and how the time allowed. There was certainly no building code, except that of longevity. But unlike the bland, monotonous housing estates of today, such apparent randomness adds a beauty and character that stimulates the senses.

There is nothing quite like experiencing history first-hand, immersing yourself in more than two millennia of communal life. Walking through narrow lanes and roads that hundreds of generations have walked before provides a unique sense of place, invokes the imagination. I try to imagine these ancient lives as people went about their business, the values they shared, a completely different kind of knowledge and understanding that they applied to their world. It was an understanding based on conceptions that we can have no inkling of today. I think of their thoughts, superstitions, their fears, their far greater appreciation of their natural world, the religious restrictions that bound their lives and of course the servitude that so many suffered for the luxury and privilege of the few.

Theirs was a life so different to our own, a life in which each person had an allotted place and status in society, a life in which very few ventured beyond the village walls, and a life that was pre-determined largely from the moment they were born. And yes, while that may not seem attractive to us today, they also possessed a certainty that we often lack. They felt safe and secure in their position, without the dislocation and anxiety-ridden social mobility that dominates much of our current lives. It is hard to pass any meaningful judgement on an era that is unlike anything we experience, an era where the meaning of knowledge itself was so incompatible with our own.

Erice is a village of a mere three hundred people. Many, such as our landlord, grew up there and remain to this day, bringing up their own young families. With so few people, the community is very cohesive. Everyone pretty well knows everyone else. Our landlord not only knows our neighbours along each side of the street, but he can tell you where they'll be and what they'll be doing at particular times of the day. As with so many towns and villages in Italy, religion provides a fairly clear framework for daily life. For these three hundred residents there are an astounding sixteen churches from different eras dedicated to a disparate collection of saints. That's one church for every nineteen people here!

A good percentage of these churches are imposing and grand in appearance, not your usual little village church. This is but a single indicator of how seriously these people take their faith. You daily see their religion symbolised around their necks in silver or gold crosses, on the large crosses of various colours that adorn front walls and doors, as well as stamped on a range of religious icons for sale in the village Co-Op. Priests with black flowing robes are a common presence in the streets and coffee shops. There is even a rather stern looking Bishop who floats across our street from time to time, gathering his white and gold, exquisitely embroidered cloak around his legs as he passes.

Our stay here is inclusive of the Easter break so it will be interesting to see just how seriously religious tradition gets. For now, we settle into our large, rustic apartment, with its spacious rooms, typical Sicilian tiled floors, a charming little balcony that overlooks the village, and a wonderful assortment of goodies that our landlord has left for us.

Erice also has more than thirty restaurants (to access summer tourists) and a tiny Co-Op, so it's time for some food shopping. The Co-Op is a goldmine. As the only one here, it services the entire village as well as tourists from Trapani and further afield. It comprises two of downstairs rooms in the owner's house, but somehow, it has everything you need. Every millimetre of shelf space is occupied, as well as items balanced on top of each other in order to fit more stock. You can hardly move for the abundance of goods, and when several people are in in the shop at the same time, you are forced to squeeze between each other on your way to one shelf or another. A middle-aged woman has apparently owned the shop for the last thirty-five years. She sits contentedly at the front desk that she has set up just inside the doorway, and collects a continuous flow of money from purchases that continue day and night. Regardless of when you visit the shop, there are customers with their arms full of groceries. I can understand her contentment.

As I said, our apartment is lovely, but like the other apartments we stay in throughout Italy, the kitchen lacks basics such as tea towels, toasters and kettles.

There is everything else you could possibly want and all of our apartments have been excellently stocked with supplies and other amenities to make life easy, even often luxurious. Kitchens have been well stocked with crockery and cutlery and condiments, but these three items continue to elude us. At a stretch I can understand the absence of toasters since many Italians prefer biscotti for breakfast rather than our more traditional preference for toast. I don't quite get the lack of kettle, since I think most people either drink coffee or tea and in places where there is no dishwasher, which in Italy is most of them, the absence of tea towels is baffling. On occasion we ask if tea towels available, but each time the owner gives us a surprised look and replies "eh, no". Twice we go further and ask how we might dry our plates and cutlery. To our great amusement, one host brings us a small bath towel for the job. Drying dishes and cutlery is apparently of no real importance here.

Back, way back

I keep rabbiting on about this, but the scope of history in these places takes some getting used to. In Australia our history of white settlement dates back only a couple of hundred years. In the USA they add another couple of hundred years to ours. We tend to think that anything older than a century or two needs to be investigated, get excited about and visited often. So, when you get to a village like Erice and walk along its two and a half-thousand-year-old Phoenician stone walls, you start to feel a bit irrelevant. The walls are extensive despite their millennia of exposure. They are high and at least a couple of feet thick, with individual stones interlocking tightly with each other to stay in place (a bit like English dry-walling). I get the feeling they will be around for another 2,500 years.

❧

Walking beside these ancient stones there is a strong desire to reach out and touch them, to connect somehow with the people who built them, who walked here before me. It helps you to understand your link in this long, long chain of human civilisation. It is a tiny link to be sure, but a necessary one if that chain is to continue.

Parading locals

Like their history, these people's religious enthusiasm also washes over you. Currently, the village is full of talk about the upcoming Easter parade; even the Americans staying in the apartment next to us are asking if we'll be at the parade. We have read that it's quite an event in Erice, having been an annual tradition since the mid-1600s. As the parade draws near there is a hive of activity around the village. Signs begin appearing in doorways and on shop windows and on the eve of the parade itself we notice a large influx of tourists from Trapani taking up all available accommodation.

By 8.am Easter parade morning, the piazza leading up the village's largest church is filling with onlookers. An hour later and the narrow streets are already teeming with people, all making their way towards the church. We decide it's time to join in and head over to find a shady place to wait. The local Mayor is being interviewed by a regional television station in front of the church, and there's a great deal of activity in and around the church itself. Participants of the parade, which, it turns out, include most of the village locals, are trying on costumes and arguing with each other about who should stand where. The priest, who appears to be in charge of the ceremony, is standing to the side, aloof and composed. Children and adults alike come up to him at regular intervals to ask for instruction. He either nods or points to a location and then waves them on.

Quite suddenly a hush of expectation descends on the crowd and the noise coming from inside the church is extinguished. The priest moves to the church's steps to take up position, looking down on the crowd. Mothers are hissing at their children to behave and stand still. The crowd has subconsciously closed in around the church and we all start jostling for the best vantage point. The procession begins with a loud trumpet call and the first of the marchers, twelve girls around 14-16 years old dressed as angels walk with a slow reverence into the piazza.

They are suitably solemn. Their mothers look on with pride. They have rehearsed this many times but still their instructor walks backwards in front of them, whispering urgent instructions. He is officious and rather pompous and by the end of the march I think most of the crowd just want to give him a slap. Then the priest begins what turns out to be a very long chant on the church steps. After a mere fifteen minutes, his young male attendant has fainted from the intense sun and building heat.

The next stage of the procession involves a float carrying large figurines of shepherds. Following this is a second float carrying the figurine of Mary Magdalene, then a third of Jesus carrying the cross and finally, a large float with Jesus dying on the cross. Each of these exceptionally heavy floats, made of solid oak, are carried by four profusely sweating men, young and old alike. Unfortunately, none of them looks like they are enjoying themselves. In fact, they have pain written all over their faces, as they struggle beneath the weight of their treasured symbols. We learn with amazement that such processions don't last the four hours that we originally thought, but actually carry on for up to twenty-four hours.

Emerging from our apartment again at around 10.pm that night we follow the sounds of the procession to a couple of blocks away. It is indeed a sorry sight. The original participants are still marching, the same poor fellows are carrying the same heavy floats, and each one is looking very much the worse for their efforts. By now, they have been trudging around these streets for approximately thirteen hours. I'm sure that before the night is out more will feint, or worse. A couple of the older men carrying floats have also had to deal with their own hefty body weight and by the look of their sweating, pale faces, will need far more than a stiff drink to recover from this ordeal. But onlookers still follow them, still cheering, drinking from flagons, smoking, laughing and enjoying to the full this Easter ritual. If I ever doubted the influence of the Catholic Church over its congregation, today I have learnt my lesson. The passion that these people have for their faith and their Church is beyond anything I have encountered. It obviously gives them great strength and purpose. It is not my role to question such commitment.

Artisanship

Another tradition for which Erice has developed a reputation is its handmade ceramics. The crafting and painting of ceramics are customs that have flowed through many generations here. Women (almost always the female line) have learnt the trade from their mothers, who have learnt from their mothers before them and most have added their own touches or refinements to individualise the craft. Beware the many tourist shops selling copies of these artefacts though. A large percentage of ceramics are produced purely for the bus tour trade, dealing in cheap tiles and figurines that are mass-produced in factories down in Trapani and occupy many of the shops along the main street. But if you can corner a local resident and extract recommendations for authentic village artisans, then you can be lucky enough to purchase some of the most beautiful, hand-crafted, intricate ceramics you will ever find.

There are the most finely detailed saucers, vases, tiles, bowls, mugs and figurines, each differently painted and shaped, each painstakingly crafted by people who have a passion for their work. The colours are a vibrant mix of blues, yellows, reds, greens and whites. Each piece has its own story, often relating to an aspect of family history or a legend of the Island, and if you find an authentic artisan, then each is individualised with no duplicates or copies. These women are intensely proud of their work and delight in relaying stories about their family's interest in ceramics and how they came to continue the tradition. Visiting these little businesses is an experience that you don't forget easily, one that enriches your visit and impression of the artisanship to be found here.

Other items for which the village is duly famous are hand woven rugs, mats, bedspreads, wall-hangings, shawls, and towels. Again, some inside knowledge is required to sidestep the cheaper imitations. We found a small shop attached to a local home in one of the village's side streets, quite a distance from the tourist route. Inside was a shy, softly spoken woman sitting at her loom, creating one of the many mats that hung gracefully around the walls of her shop. She gave a courteous nod before returning to her craft. I asked if all the items in the shop were made by her and she replied in very broken English that of course they were, the craft had been in her family for four generations.

She proudly showed us photos of her mother, grandmother and great grandmother, sitting in the same shop, making the same mats and rugs that she is now crafting. Guiding us through the complexities of the loom, the woman demonstrates in slow motion how it operates, drawing on and weaving the wool in its systematic, rhythmic way. Wendy and I marvel at the patience and skill required for this craft. We also can't help noticing the woman's gnarled hands with large, swollen knuckles and chafed fingers, despite her relatively young age of only forty-five or so. This hour within the shop, talking to this quiet, proud artisan, allows a tiny insight into what it means to respect and nurture a family tradition, and a craft that has been a hallmark of this village for centuries. As with the ceramic shop, we leave with a beautiful handmade product that represents all the passion and skill of these artisans, something we will treasure always.

Night wanderings

Exploring Erice by evening is perhaps the most entrancing time of all. Making our way to the very top of the village we are treated to a 360-degree view that captures much of Sicily. During the day, the view is breathtaking, particularly early morning with the sunrise reflecting on a deep crimson and turquoise ocean below. But at night, you look out across the plains with the thousand twinkling lights of houses far below to the dark hulks of mountains in the distance. You feel a cool breeze rising from a vast ocean, and listen to soft birdsong as the night closes in. The castle and churches are floodlit, showcasing them against a darkening sky. The serenity is absolute. The village below us is quiet, voices have softened, music has stopped, life is slowing down. Now it is just us and these ancient formations, witnessing the close of another day – one more in a long, era-filled line of such days.

Looking back towards the *Mother Church*, you understand why it represents the centrepiece of Erice. Majestic at night with its stone walls bathed in soft light it stands as a beacon of these people's deep faith. The grand bell tower, white marble roof and stone taken from the Castle of Venus at the top of the village, sitting just outside the magnificent Balio Gardens. The castle dates back to the 12th century and sits on the original site of the Temple by the same name, which survived each of the invading empires. From here, you can take the winding pathway through the gardens, which at night are eerily beautiful. You can walk through to the castle beyond and then the lookout on the point. Or you can head in the opposite direction to arrive at the Pepoli Tower, a haunting edifice from which views are just as inspiring, taking in many of Erice's medieval forts and defence walls.

After almost two hours of wandering in this evocative place we eventually stroll back to the apartment and join our American neighbours on the balcony. The four of us relax into some low-slung chairs and open several bottles of Chianti while swapping tales of our day. They are a middle-aged couple, she a delight, interesting, interested and endlessly polite. He is a fellow who is immediately friendly but gives the impression he is trying just a little too hard. It is always fascinating to hear others' impressions of the place you are in and their own particular travel priorities. Like us, this couple attempt to immerse themselves in a limited number of places and really try to understand the local community and culture of each place. So, we have an evening of swapping stories and shared travel interests, of hearing about the expectations they brought with them and whether they have been fulfilled. These two are seasoned travellers to Italy so provide a wealth of knowledge and inside hints. An evening of laughter, eating and drinking follows, an evening in which we reflect on this captivating village and the seductive effect it's had on us. Erice will not be easily forgotten. It is with some sadness that we count down the last few days of our stay.

Chapter Six: Sea of Temples

Back into our tiny Fiat we climb the winding coastal roads towards Agrigento, or to be exact, the Scala dei Turchi ("Stair of the Turks"), which is a seaside "resort" near Agrigento. There is only one reason for this leg of the journey and it's not the seaside "resort". Driving into the area our road hugs the coastline, with the magnificent Mediterranean on our left, sparkling in its expanse. On our right, there is a flat, nothingness. In terms of services Scala dei Turchi boasts little more than a couple of restaurants which have seen better days, a crooked, yellow and white gelato stand on the side of the road that also sells beer, and the "resort" in which we are booked for the next two nights.

White noise

The car park at our accommodation is already full. Of course it is, it's the only hotel in town. The single-story accommodation wing is a vast expanse of white with blue trim. The adjoining restaurant is also white with blue trim. The reception complex is white with blue trim, and the pool house is white with blue trim. They are obviously attempting to exaggerate the Mediterranean *feel* of the place. Inside our hotel room, *stark* is the only adjective that comes to mind. It is very clean and new and exclusively white. I mean *everything* is white. White floors, walls, beds, benches, bathroom, ceilings, even the television. It almost hurts the eyes. I test the fridge but there is no sign of life. I call reception to report it and their simple and effective response is to come over and switch it with the one in the next room. I suspect, when the next people check in there, reception will be getting another call. This fridge has probably been doing the rounds for some time.

Very quickly, we need a break from the pervasive white, so head out to the gelato stand to buy some beer before walking down on to the beach below, to view the legendary "White Cliffs". Everyone else in Scala dei Turchi is there too. The cliffs are formed by a mixture of limestone, and sedimentary rock called *mari*, and when the sun reflects on their face they transform into an incandescent white. This, against the deep blue of the Mediterranean Sea provides a spectacular, contrasting display. The natural beauty that we encounter in remote places like this so often takes you by surprise. Sicily, I'm discovering to my delight, has a rich bounty of such places. And as yet, they don't feature too prominently on the European tourist trail, which has to be a good thing.

Later, it's time to try the only dining room in town - the resort restaurant - which unlike the hotel rooms, is delightful, even though again, pure white throughout. The food is very reasonably priced and of excellent quality. The service is impeccable, not just in efficiency but in attention and friendliness. The waiters stand at a little distance watching for any sign at all that we may, at some stage, be vaguely in need of something. As soon as we glance in their direction the Maitre D' snaps his fingers for one of his underlings to rush to our service. These people seem to love us just being here. They can't do enough for our happiness. Gluten free options are extensive, and when they don't have a *gf* substitute, they will offer to make something especially for me. You just don't get that type of attention very often. The wine, of course, is mainly Sicilian and therefore not my favourite tipple. But when the only alternative is gelato and beer you make the best of it.

Marvelling at Monuments

Next morning is time to head out for the real reason we're here – the *Valley of the Temples*, just outside Agrigento. Directions from our GPS are somewhat confusing. Wendy driving, with me reading maps is even more confusing. The GPS tells us to turn right in 200 metres but for some reason Wendy interprets that as 'turn right now'. We do, and drive right into the front yard of a local house, with mum, dad and a child outside looking curiously at the unexpected visitors who drive their car right up to the door. They are even more surprised, when we smile and wave before doing a three-point turn and quickly heading back onto the road. The tension in the car by this time has escalated. After several more wrong turns and an inadvertent switch onto the wrong side of the road, the atmosphere becomes positively heated. Wendy is flustered, I'm in a lot of trouble and the GPS will soon be on its way out the window. I foolishly remind Wendy that she seems to have trouble judging distances and tends to turn too early. I'm confronted with a stare that would curdle milk so immediately busy myself with picking lint from my jumper.

After an extended period of judicious silence, the car park for *Valley of the Temples* is finally located. And what a destination it is! We're confronted with acre upon acre of some of the most exquisitely preserved Greek ruins in existence. Remains of large villas, a total of eight temples, including those of Heracles, Concordia, Demeter and Zeus, as well as numerous burial sites, bath houses, giant Telamones, and meeting houses are cast far and wide across the 1,300-acre park. The entire day until late in the evening is spent wandering among these Greek, Roman and Medieval relics, marvelling at the details and level of preservation, at the overt symbolism embedded in each monument, trying to imagine ways in which they were used and the meanings ascribed.

Agrigento was originally one of the major cities of Magna Graecia during Ancient Greece's most illustrious age. It dates back to around 580BC, one of the last major Greek colonies in Sicily to be settled. Them during the first Punic War in 262BC, the Romans invaded and pillaged the city of Agrigento, relegating the entire population to slavery. It was fought over again 200 years later when Rome and Carthage contested Sicilian territory before its citizens eventually received Roman citizenship around 40BC. Agrigento fell victim to multiple minor empires before, with the rest of Sicily, coming under Norman control in AD 1087. The archaeological park now abounds with sumptuous reminders of this city's turbulent past.

History and pop music
What becomes apparent to us in this place, is that Sicilians must have such an abundance of archaeological history and in so many locations that their reverence is diminished. People are allowed to and do, walk all over these relics, children playing, others sitting on them to have lunch or their photo taken, even one man with his towel spread, radio on sunbaking. Very few of the relics are roped off but it makes little difference if they are, as people simply step over and continue their activities.

Frustratingly, we have to wait to take photos of a temple for fifteen minutes, while four schoolgirls dance around on top of it, striking poses and taking countless 'selfies'. They show no interest in the actual relic, just the number of different poses they can strike for their phone cameras. There are no officials to stop or admonish them, and no notice taken by any of the locals. The perverse juxtaposition between these millennia-old relics and a twenty-first century mobile device designed to exaggerate our own self-importance strikes a deep chord of despair. It appears that for this young generation, even the plight of human civilisation and history pales to insignificance beside the latest cheap imitation of life.

But for those with more than a couple of neurons, you can't help but be deeply affected by the sheer historical distance that Sicilians' roots extend. Five, six, even thousand years of human civilisation come to life, diminishing your own meagre life span to a microcosm. But it's a history so complex and intriguing that you realise your own space in human evolution *does* have a point. You are part of this great journey into the past and the future. You maintain the link by playing your tiny but vital role. History and archaeology can provide a treasure of ancestral meaning, if only we take some time to appreciate the riches left behind.
***

It had been a long day strolling around 1300 acres of monuments under a deep blue sky and relentless sunshine. Typically, I had left the hotel that morning without either a hat or sunscreen, expecting only a gentle sprinkling of UV rays for this time of year. And typically, I had returned from our excursion burnt and bloodshot-eyed. In weeks and weeks of travel through Italy so far, we have had exactly 90 minutes of rain. That was a sudden downpour in a thunderstorm that cleared as quickly as it arrived and returned the day to brilliant sun. We haven't even had clouds, just day after day of blue skies and eight hours of sun. As a result, I'm a permanent shade of red from the neck up and even more frustrated by my inability to learn from the previous day(s) of sunscreen-free roaming. For now, however, it is dinner, one or two quick beers to cool that sunburn, before packing up for our next leg of the trip.

Chapter Seven: Oranges for the Blessed

There are mixed feelings in our car as we head back out on to the great Italian highways. Wendy is excited but I can't quite generate the same level of enthusiasm. That being the case, I think it best to resume my judicious silence until something scenic distracts us both. This is a trip after all, in which we will both need to compromise from time to time. And to be honest, Wendy has been more than generous in compromises so far. I just have to get over myself and focus on yet another beautiful, sunny day. Besides, when I think about it, there is no particular reason for my unenthusiastic outlook. It's a feeling based on nothing much at all. I have no actual knowledge of Taormina. The town just doesn't fit comfortably into my idealistic notion of what Sicily should be. But all my pre-conceived notions have been wrong so far so why would this town be any different? It is also Wendy's anniversary present to us both so I need to show some grace or as an old friend would say, give myself a swift kick in the butt.

Wrong turns

The omens are less than supportive, however. After a series of wrong turns, followed by subsequent arguments and accusations, we make a final wrong turn into a little lane that takes us straight onto the beach. Faced with sand and waves rolling in our direction, more accusations and hateful comments about the GPS follow. We even debate burying it at sea. A period of silent exasperation follows, while we contemplate our pathetic navigation skills, then Fiat retraces its route back onto what we hope is the road to Taormina.

With memories of our approach to Erice, we urge our little car into climbing again. The roads are long and steep and incredibly confusing. Lanes run off in multiple directions with no sensible signs on where we're supposed to be heading. Traffic is also quite heavy and the Italian preference for fast driving and cutting corners allows us little time to make rational driving choices. We basically take a turn wherever there's a reasonable gap in the traffic, whether we're supposed to head that way or not.

I have a bright idea of calling our new host for some clarification on which road is our best option. Her typically Italian response is: "Just head up the hill. I'll see you soon", and with that the phone goes dead. A blue Alpha Romeo that had been about 300 metres ahead and which we'd been following, suddenly appears from behind a stone wall coming back towards us. "Oh my God! I give up" shouts Wendy before yanking the steering wheel and sending us onto the gravel at the roadside. She rips the handbrake on, jumps out of the car and stands staring at me. We also now notice the other cars we'd been following also coming back towards us. This godforsaken road just circles the wall at the top for no apparent reason.

In desperation, I run across both lanes to a group of road-workers sitting on the barrier, taking in the ocean view. The casual answer to my query is to "cut across that road ahead and in just one mile you arrive at Taormina". I try to point out that there is a large traffic island between us and *that road.* "No matter, you drive over the island". To my surprise, my ever law-abiding and cautious wife does just that. Our car crunches its way over the traffic island and we're on our way, with a little self-satisfied smirk creeping around the corners of Wendy's mouth. I have learned that there are many ways to do things in Italy, many of them unconventional. You just do what is necessary.

Views from Above
We unload our bags onto the balcony of a stunning villa with uninterrupted views of the Ionian Sea (I begin to realise what a lavish anniversary gift this actually is) and then immediately jump back into the car to return it to the rental yard. I have to say, we are fairly eager to off-load this little four-wheel companion and return to pedestrian mode. There will be fewer wrong directions and less arguing. Of course, being Sicily, the car rental office is closed. I check my watch and it is midday. I was told on the phone that there would be someone in attendance until 1.30pm, forgetting that *time* doesn't mean a lot here. Wendy rings the assistant who explains that she has decided to visit her sister in another town and won't be back until 4.pm. Leaving the fiat in a car-park across the road,

we walk back to the apartment and take possession of our dream for the next few days.

And what a place it is! It was a stone's throw from the town centre, but in a quiet side lane. To take full advantage of those views I mentioned, there's a beautiful, large balcony with lemon and grapefruit trees and seating for about twenty people. The villa is finished in traditional terracotta tiles and bright blue wooden shutters on the windows. You couldn't get more Sicilian. Inside the place is spacious, tastefully and expensively decorated, stocked with everything we could ever want and boasting the most comfortable lounge I have ever had the pleasure of sitting in. Each large window in the lounge, kitchen and bedroom has views of the sea below. The rooms are large with beautiful furniture, and there's a luxurious air about the place that instantly envelopes us. The day's frustration quickly evaporates as we settle into bliss. I realise how much thought and expense Wendy had put into this present and instantly regret my little rants throughout the day.

Taormina is a little difficult for me to describe. From its hilltop perch it commands stunning views in all directions. The sea surrounds us and the coastline below is dramatic in its contours. Clouds punctuate the views below, accentuating the physical landscape and bringing it more clearly into focus. In the background Mt Etna smokes and smoulders. It is clearly visible from the main street of Taormina and provides a spectacular contrast to views of the lush green hillside and vast ocean in the other direction. The narrow roads are lined with wonderful little cafes and shops selling the town's wares, but in high season they are populated with hordes of tourists. Fortunately, we are here in March so crowds are not as much of an issue. The roads themselves lead from one historical site to another. You can visit a myriad of Roman relics, including an entire amphitheatre, as well as Norman castles and medieval villas.

The Corvaja Palace, for example, is a fine specimen of medieval architecture, built in the 10th century and housing the Sicilian parliament in the 15th. It sits in Taormina's delightful Piazza Badia. Another fascinating site is the Palazzo Duchi

S. Stefano, which you see as soon as you enter Taormina through the large, arched stone gateway. Again Medieval, having been built in the 14th century, it belonged to one of Sicily's and in fact Italy's leading aristocratic families, the Dukes of Santo Stefano. The palace itself sits resplendent in its manicured grounds, priding itself as one of the most popular sites in the town.

Or, if exquisite gardens are more your thing, then don't miss the Villa Communale. Set amongst Taormina's lush public park, the villa is surrounded by exotic plants and miniature architecture, giving the place a fairy tale atmosphere. The gardens were created by a genteel English woman -Florence Trevelyan - whose own personal history and the purpose of this garden are very much intertwined. Born in 1852, Florence was a member of Britain's aristocracy, but her father committed suicide when she was only two. She and her mother moved to Northumberland and established a range of unique gardens before, as a young adult, she was rumoured to become the mistress of Price Edward of Wales. According to legend, the Royal Family was not particularly fussed on her dalliances with the young Prince and encouraged her, with a significant cash incentive, to leave English shores. She accepted their offer and travelled Europe before finally settling in Taormina, never to return to England. There she added to her already considerable fortune by marrying Taormina's mayor, who was also happened to be one of the town's wealthiest doctors. With lots of spare time and more money than she could ever hope to spend, she set about creating beautiful gardens through the importation of exotic plants. Today, her legacy remains one of the truly imaginative gardens of Sicily.

Playground

Narrowness is a defining characteristic of the streets and laneways in this hilltop oasis. Each lane is at most, -a single car width, and by that, I mean a *small* car. If two cars meet, the last to arrive will have to reverse to a leeway or connecting lane into which it can manoeuvre out of the way. Villas and apartments lining these lanes are almost exclusively stone, often four, five or six hundred years in age, and sometimes older, reaching back as far as the early Medieval period. They are beautifully maintained. People take pride in their properties and obviously have the money required to look after them.

Unlike many Sicilian towns, there is no sign of poverty in Taormina. It is often referred to as the Sicilian French Riviera, with the Lonely Planet guide describing it as "sophisticated, chic (with some) ... serious wealth". Although a playground of the rich, however, Taormina remains beautifully unspoilt, tastefully mixing expensive shopping and a saturation of brand names with a pristine natural environment. It is also surrounded by challenging walking tracks, but those who persevere will always be rewarded with breathtaking views. In fact, many claim it as having one of the world's best views. I am in no hurry to argue with this.

The town itself is sizable and incorporates all the retail, service and accommodation options of a thriving settlement. It has approximately 10,000 inhabitants, but numbers fluctuate drastically between winter and summer, as well as between weekends and weekdays, so official statistics are pretty fluid. Being in a position to host the 2017 G7 forum, however, is a fairly good indicator of just how accessible, well-provisioned and desirable the place it is.

Before about 10.am you can walk through quiet, undisturbed laneways getting to know your way around and uncovering some of the more obscure attractions. You can visit the tiny delicatessens, sampling some good Italian coffee and world-famous pastries. If you get out even earlier you can be the only one about. This is my favourite time, as you have the place to yourself. You can stroll at will, take in the solitude, lean over the wall at the edge of town and take in truly stunning views, wander into one or two of the Medieval convents that still stand proudly, or just stretch out in the early morning sun and feel your body slowly, luxuriously responding to the warmth of another spring day. You really need to experience this early morning tranquillity because the closer to noon you get the more tourists that descend on the place and the streets suddenly fill with day-trippers.

Despite the obvious tourism and commercial vibe of the village, you can't help but fall in love with Taormina. Although the streets can fill quickly with people, they add to the vibrancy and energy of the town. There is a buzz, a feel-good atmosphere that follows you through the streets, into the cafes, along the lanes that wind their way backwards and forwards across the main street, leading you into mysterious little nooks.

Seizing Solitude

But when it all gets a bit much, we like to escape back to our quiet and luxurious villa, an act that has a special resonance given that we can choose whether to join the excitement of the tourists, for how long, or not at all. It seems we can have the best of both worlds –crowded, vibrant streets, or absolute peace and quiet. Over the coming days, we find ourselves alternating constantly between these two worlds, enjoying our fill of each. It is wonderful to enjoy the town at different times of the day. To come out in the early morning and experience it without any human interaction, to walk among the crowds at lunch-time, joining in the happy jostling, and then to come back out at sunset to witness the scenery of a hilltop town, ending its day among landscapes of exquisite beauty. As dusk descends, the colours soften and change their hue, coating natural and manmade landscapes in an altogether different tenor of light. Mount Etna sits brooding quietly in the distance. It had erupted only 10 days before our arrival and ash smoke still oozes from its crater, shrouding the volcano in a grey blanket night and day.

I think dusk can be the most peaceful, evocative time of all. It is when you truly understand the beauty that a place offers, its moods, its timeless history, its sense of permanence. It is reassuring. Another day has passed and now the town will rest and cleanse itself in preparation for a new dawn. The heat has left for the day. The narrow streets that were crowded just a few hours ago become quiet avenues of serenity, of contemplation.

History on the hilltop

What has recently been a playground for the likes of John Steinbeck, Greta Garbo, Elizabeth Taylor and Oscar Wilde, Taormina began its life as a resort town in the first couple of centuries BCE, when Roman Senators took their vacations in here.

Although most record Taormina's beginning at the 4th century BCE when its wealth and religious significance caught the attention of the outside world, the town's roots can actually be traced back a further seven hundred and thirty odd years. Like the rest of Sicily, the town has had more invaders than they care to think about. The Greek (in 392BCE), Roman, Byzantine, Arab, Norman, French and Spanish empires have all had a go, with invasions spanning almost two thousand years. Under Arab rule from AD 960 the town became a learning centre for the High Arts and Sciences, including philosophy and mathematics, drawing scholars from Greece, Rome and the Arab world. Such a scholarly flavour only enhanced the lure of Taormina as a Mediterranean playground and the town continued to prosper right through the new millennium, including its eventual overthrow of the French in the 1200s and its later political elevation to seat of the Sicilian Parliament. (vii)

The Spanish invasion in 1538 is the most recent and, at least to begin with, was a good deal friendlier than previous conquests. But alas, as they settled into their new environment, they began to unleash their own brand of torment and misery. In addition to a sizable number of Spanish immigrants flowing into Sicily and Taormina, the Empire also exported its own special version of religious fanaticism in the form of the Spanish Inquisition. Wreaking wide-scale havoc as early as the 1480s the Spanish set about purging Sicilians of their "heretical beliefs", insisting they convert to Catholicism and confess their sins, or suffer the consequences. As was their habit, although it came as somewhat of a shock to the native Taorminians, the Spanish also managed to locate and put to death a number of previously unknown witches.

For the next quarter of a century Taormina suffered much like the rest of Europe as fervent bigotry brought misery, torture and even death to the locals. And, as has been common practice since almost the beginning of time, Jews within the town were singled out for particular attention. With their property and worldly goods confiscated and their beliefs outlawed, the small Jewish population was given the choice of either being expelled from the town permanently, or a death of their choosing. Even including this bleak and shameful period, each conqueror has left unique cultural flavours so that today, Taormina has a rich and eclectic past to draw upon.

On Guard

Somewhat incongruously, this serene locality, with its historic architecture and relics, its perpetual holiday atmosphere, and its removal from the rest of the world, is also populated with military personnel. Armed with semi-automatic weapons, pistols and knives, they stand guard at each entrance to the main piazza as well as roaming the town in pairs. It is somewhat off-putting, even ominous, while also oddly reassuring, given global events at present. I suppose the discomfort is that they are always present and noticeable, and at odds with the natural tranquillity. You can be looking at the spectacular view in one direction and then turn in the other to see a semi-automatic weapon, only feet from you and pointing in your general direction.

In Italy, it seems, there is now quite a lot of armed response at hand. A 2015 article in the Guardian states that a national deployment of 4,800 troops will guard just about everything of national significance. Five hundred alone are stationed in Rome, while monuments, major tourist sites, synagogues, some schools, cathedrals and significant archaeological sites around Italy will also receive their allocation of firepower. And don't even try to count the number guarding the Vatican.

It is a reminder of the cauldron that Europe has become, a reminder that safety is rarely a human right. The military personnel are also very aware of this. On one occasion, we are standing just feet away from two armed soldiers with everything as it should be, when a hundred metres to our right loud yelling between several men breaks the normal rhythm of things. Instantly the two soldiers spin in the direction of the noise with hands going straight to their guns.

The yelling subsides and things return to normal. The two soldiers watch closely for half a minute more then finally relax. Their immediate reaction, however, demonstrates just how prepared they are for sudden violence. Again, fear and reassurance compete at a personal level.

The military presence is something we never quite get used to in Italy. We expect it in Rome, a large, busy city full of national monuments, as well as hosting EU dignitaries on a continual basis, but the presence is pretty well everywhere. In each place where crowds may be expected there is a very obvious presence. They are always heavily armed and ready for response. Sometimes, it seems everyone wants to have a go at protecting you. Often, we will arrive at a cathedral or national monument to find representatives from the *Polizia di Stato* (state police), the *Carabinieri* (some kind of military police), local *Polizia,* as well as actual soldiers all jostling for position and authority.

The soldiers always seem to be in charge and demonstrate their superiority by effectively ignoring the other forces. The local and state police can appear confused about their role, spending a lot of time wandering around, inspecting their cars or visiting local shops. But it is the *Carabinieri* that I love. No matter which monument they are guarding or what their role is *supposed* to be their conduct never changes. They lean on their car bonnets, smoking one of their Italian Toscana cigars, usually taking more than a mild interest in pretty young women passing by, and chatting happily with anyone who cares to talk with them.

Interestingly, about 70% of the nation's *Carabinieri* are recruited from Southern Italy, and mostly Sicily and Calabria. Coincidentally, these are the two regions from which Italy's notorious Mafia originate and remain to this day. If you have read anything of Italy's Cosa Nostra gangs, you will have heard of the *Carabinieri.* They feature among the Mafia's opponents in newspapers, academic studies, crime novels, and of course, major movies including the Godfather series. In many, the Carabinieri are also portrayed as slow and rather dim-witted, easily outmanoeuvred by local mob bosses. Similarly, there is a whole repertoire of

Carabinieri jokes that Italians love to regale each other with and which usually portray the police as somewhat intellectually challenged. Nevertheless, these, together with Italy's other police and military forces are a constant reminder of the determination to meet terrorism head on and hopefully their years of dealing with the country's Mafia has taught them a few tricks.

Tantalising tastebuds

Thinking along more innocent lines, Taormina reminds us again of our initial enthusiasm for all foods Italian. The food has been one of the great joys of this Italian adventure. Its freshness and inconsiderable cost are a reminder of what a wonderful experience food can be. We are eager to sample from the orange and grapefruit trees growing on our villa's front terrace. I am not particularly keen on citrus fruits, generally eating them only when no other fruit is available, or when an occasional, random urge takes hold of me. With the deliciously ripe oranges hanging low from our tree, one of those urges strikes now. I pick one and cut it up on a plate. It is full and juicy and quite simply the most divine orange I have ever, ever tasted. In fact, it is one of the most delicious *foods* I had ever eaten. I simply didn't realise oranges could taste this good. Wendy tries the grapefruit next on her cereal and exclaims; "Oh my God. This is so good". After these first samples, a good proportion of the fruit is demolished over the next few days. Yes, it is a desire driven entirely by greed. But we are so addicted by now that we are beyond caring. They can't grow fruit this good and expect people to leave it alone. It will certainly be hard, going back to cold-stored supermarket fruit after this.

Delving deep

As if this town doesn't have enough to offer, there is a well-preserved Greek theatre yet to be explored at the edge of the main thoroughfare, perhaps half a mile from town. We set off with cameras to investigate. We have been saturated with ancient ruins for much of our Italian odyssey, but as a history buff I don't think you can ever get enough of ruins and relics. The theatre turns out to be a very well preserved one indeed. Although it has workman climbing all over it in preparation for the evening's theatrical performance, we are able to walk through its entirety. There are large sections of the original semi-circle seating still intact, in stepped gradient looking down upon what would have been the stage. The original covered walkways surrounding the theatre are still evident, as is the back wall of the theatre, shielding it from weather and perhaps uninvited onlookers.

You have to stand a little while and try to imagine the momentous events that occurred here. These theatres were, under Greek rule, dedicated to the regular philosophical debates and moots in which the great orators, debaters and logicians of Socrates', Aristotle's and Plato's ilk taught students in the art of debate and intellectual discourse. These were places of great learning, milestones in the march of modern civilisation. You feel humbled to stand in such a theatre, to understand what has transpired here two and three millennia before. People entering now still become quiet and contemplative, with some understanding of just what a significant place this is.

The Theatre's more recent history, the five hundred years between 200 BCE and AD 300 under Roman rule, provides a stark contrast in activity and development. For the Romans it was as far removed from a seat of intellectual debate as you could get. They turned it, and many more like it into arenas of purely lustful entertainment, where slave gladiators fought each other and wild animals for audience entertainment. Often, they just fought for pure survival. There was little learning under the Roman rule, but rather, barbaric indulgence under what was gradually becoming a debauched and morally corrupt empire.

Gladiatorial games usually began with three pairs of gladiators fighting to the death, after which the winning pair would go on to fight newcomers or the latest wild bear or lion that had been caught. Blood lust was the key ingredient and the major drawcard for emperors and commoners alike. Anyone classed as a gladiator lost all status as a human being under Roman rule and swore an oath to die by the sword if not mauled or burned first. On occasion, the arenas were even flooded with water so that mock naval battles could be orchestrated. Sometimes, there would be as many as six thousand crew members with their boats all in the one arena, an event that would draw thousands of spectators and be promoted as a special event on the social calendar. Although these battles were promoted as "mock", there were plenty of real deaths and as much violence and blood as could be organised for the local emperor's entertainment.

When not used for fighting, legend has it that these arenas were often popular sites of demonic rituals, accompanied by drunken orgies and other debauched behaviour, although much of this "testimony" arose within strict anti-pagan movements and later, the Catholic Church. But it is fair to say that the arenas were used for a variety of purposes, many involving prostitutes and brothels and others considered acutely distasteful by today's standards. Such "entertainment" is usually symbolic of an empire in the throes of degeneration and decay. In that respect, the Roman Empire was following a traditional path.

How's the vino?
I think the only thing not overly enjoyable in Taormina is something I haven't really enjoyed since arriving in Sicily. Sicilian wine. Like Italians the land over, Sicilians take great pride in their wines and try to foist them on you at every opportunity. But Sicilian wine is not Chianti or a Barolo.

Yesterday I entered one of Taormina's artisan shops that specialised in a gourmet range of Sicilian olives, cheeses, pate, salami and "exclusive" Sicilian wines. The sales-woman spent almost fifteen minutes attempting to indoctrinate me into the "mystical spell "of what she referred to as Sicily's *icon wines*. Well, through my studies, I know a bit about icon wines and had yet to see Sicilian wines among them. I was looking forward to what she was going to come up with. She asked me if I'd tried any of the wines on offer and what I thought of them. I replied, perhaps a little too rudely, that I thought Sicily had many excellent agricultural products, but wine is not one of them". She gave me a shocked look and simply walked away.

Sicilian wine is grown mostly in the lowlands, a place you should never attempt to grow vines. These vines are crammed together, with no evident pruning or canopy management. They are often grown on the south sides of hills, in clay soil, a soil notoriously bad for drainage – in fact, everything a vine hates. As a result, the wines tend to be sweet, a bit one-dimensional and fairly unbalanced. They can taste rather like liquid lollies. But the catch is that in Sicily, that's all that's available.

After reading the stats on Sicily's wine it all makes terrible sense. Sicily specialises in *bulk wine*. For those who are not familiar with this term, it refers to the stuff that goes into *goon bags*, or casks. It is all about getting the most alcohol for the least expense. Giacosa, one of France's most renowned oenologists, describes these wines as "strong, rustic, heavy and oxidised". (viii) In wine terms, *oxidised* means the wine has gone bad, having been exposed to too much oxygen while producing and cellaring. In short, it has died. This leaves it with an unpleasant taste and the smell of unwashed socks. To make matters worse, the wines are not at all cheap, in fact, they are out of all proportion to the quality of the wine. But, like everywhere in Italy, every shop, no matter how small, or what type of shop it is, sells wine. No matter where you go, you are never without wine, which, if only it was decent, would be a wonderful thing.

Chapter Eight: Steel tracks to Syracuse

It is time to begin the final stage of our journey. And, it is with real sadness that this affluent, beautiful hilltop town is being left behind. Taormina has been far more than I expected, as has so much of Italy. It has charmed, entranced and seduced. It leaves us yearning for more, to remain, to continue absorbing its daily delights. Moving through this hypnotic island, with its natural beauty, its vigorous, generous people and its ancient wonders, I find all pre-conceived ideas are simply swept away. The island of Sicily is so utterly different from what you might expect, so compelling in its raw magnetism that you cannot help but be bewitched. This land has found its way deep into my soul. It has changed the way I think, what I value. But mostly, it has reminded me of how truly beguiling life can be, if you just allow yourself to accept.

****

We wait on the immaculate Taormina railway platform for our train to Ortygia. Locals, as usual, are acutely interested, and stroll up to talk to us, to ask where we're from, where we are going, how long we have been here, and what we think of the place. They provide bits and pieces of their own lives in a strangely humble way, apologising for their imperfect English. They're polite, friendly and seem pretty happy with their lot in life. They put up with their country's many imperfections with cheer and goodwill, shrugging their shoulders and smiling away problems. There is a lot we can learn from them. Many of us are more than willing to pass judgement on foreign contemporaries. There is a certain parochialism and insularity that surfaces when we comment on "outsiders". It's a self-righteousness that compares other people and systems to our own and always seems to find them wanting. For some illogical reason, we tend to believe that what *we* have is the best available, a template by which all others should be judged. When we encounter difference the first reaction tends to be one of criticism and derision, rather than acceptance. It is a sad reflection on how myopic we can be.

Often, such myopia is demonstrated when discussing political or legal systems. We criticise the French, for example, for their handling of potential criminals, their need to demonstrate *proof of innocence*. We criticise Italians for their detaining powers, use of protective arms and a chaotic justice system. We laugh at the American political system for no other reason than we can't understand it. Australians advocate the 'one true' Westminster system of government, even though, if we knew anything of history, we'd realise that ours is not a true Westminster system at all, but rather a *mongrelisation* of several different systems in which we have failed to even legislate a basic mantle of human rights.

But back to Taormina. We're now boarding our very clean train. The next two hours are spent hugging a picturesque coastline before turning inland through a number of towns and villages in varying degrees of poverty. Few of the towns match the level of affluence to be found in Taormina, but a number appear to be in extreme poverty, with derelict housing, rusted-out cars scattered across backyards, many apparently unemployed youths in various stages of boredom, and a general despair that lingers in the streets. In this south-eastern region the unemployment rate climbs as high as 45%, the highest by far in Italy, and as manufacturing and construction move northwards, the situation is only becoming worse. Around 75% of the land is still used for agriculture but even in this sector, returns are diminishing through EU "balancing" programs and bureaucratic restrictions, as well as monopolies by the largest landowners.

In addition, organised crime here is back to the levels witnessed in the 1950s and 60s, with a hierarchy of crime gangs controlling everything from fuel and food, to building works, unionised labour, and most transport channels. Government reforms to trade and commerce are routinely sabotaged and neutralised by the crime bosses. Not a lot happens down here without some form of criminal involvement, and a vibrant black economy extends through each sector of business.

Geographically, the country is now levelling out with a *sameness* and monotony taking hold. Yet the trip is again a credit to Italian public infrastructure. The train is fast and quiet, and service is impeccable. The timetable is adhered to, with departure and arrival times exactly as stated in the schedule.

Chapter Nine: Seashore Dreaming

Arrival in the small city of Syracuse, is slightly disorientating after Taormina, as the character, perhaps the spirit of the place – I'm not sure how to describe it – is quite unlike the rest of Sicily. Emerging from the station I feel that we have entered a sleepy, languorous mid-twentieth century town. There are few cars, the pace is slow, shops have an old-fashioned feel to them and for a so-called city it's very, very quiet. Geographically, Syracuse is small. The whole city can be visited on foot and judging by the lack of cars, most people do this. Yet at the height of its power in 400BCE, a time when it was claimed to be the most powerful city of the ancient world, Syracuse was large and intimidating with a population approaching 300,000.

Those times have passed. It seems that the city now rests, enjoying its twilight years as a place of serenity and historical reflection. There is still a distinctly Greek *feel* to the place, despite these original occupants having been in residence some 2,700 years ago. It still carries much of the Greek flavour through its amphitheatres, architecture and even cuisine, and lays claims to one of the greatest mathematicians of all time, the Greek born Archimedes. Syracuse is rich in its ancient history and culture and unlike many cities today, it celebrates its heritage through an adherence to strong cultural roots. The city is now a UNESCO World Heritage site, and its location, fronting the beautiful turquoise of the Ionian Sea, provides an oasis of tranquillity and relaxation for weary travellers. For us though, it serves as a wonderful, ancient gateway to our final destination, its intimately close neighbour Ortygia.

Ortygia is simply the really old part of the city, reached by a bridge connecting it to the rest of Syracuse. It is a separate and tiny island of cobbled streets, five-hundred-year-old stone villas, and exquisite piazzas. The island itself has a total landmass measuring just one kilometre long by a mere six hundred metres wide. Such tiny measurements ensure that the available land is crowded. And, like the rest of Syracuse, it is securely locked into a 1950s-time warp.

The entrance to Ortygia hosts an impressive archaeological park in which, amazingly, the remains of both Greek *and* Roman theatres are nestled as well as the Temple of Apollo. Quite a boast for any city. The Temple can be traced back to the 700s BCE and suffered several reconfigurations as the Greek, Byzantine, Muslim and Norman Empires adopted it for their own brands of faith. Three hundred metres down the cobbled street visitors can witness a truly biblical wonder. Flowing into a sunken pond surrounded by stone walls is a constant stream of fresh water from under Ortygia's streets. More importantly though, it is one of the only places in the world in which papyrus thrives. The papyrus in this particular pond was transported here from Egypt in the second and third centuries BCE. Those same papyrus roots support the plants that grow there today. The pond also represents the place where legend has it that the Greek God Alpheus fell for the scantily clad, in fact naked, Arethusa while she sunned herself. Here, after begging for help she was thoughtfully turned into a continuous water source for the city, benefitting pretty well everyone.

But there is far more to Ortygia then ancient remains and Greek legends. Visitors here are strongly discouraged from bringing their car with them, as most streets are too narrow for comfortable driving and parking space is a rare luxury. This makes the old city a pedestrian paradise, particularly as it's an island you can circumnavigate in 30 minutes. Your wandering will inevitably take you past any number of street markets, where you can purchase tonight's dinner from cold meats, fresh cuts, a full range of locally grown fruit and vegetables, freshly caught fish, crab, sea urchins, and just about any other seafood you can think of, including some you would rather not. Other stalls sell clothes, shoes, hats and table after table of junk. The markets open at 7.am each morning and usually stay in operation until about 1 or 2.pm, depending on the crowds. They are a hive of activity with stall owners and customers haggling over prices and size of servings, bartering between other stall owners, the loud interruption of mopeds weaving between pedestrians and the delicious smells of frying whitebait or oysters being prepared while you wait.

Sublime Simplicity

You can wander for hours taking in the sights and sounds and smells of this glorious little community. Getting lost is not really an option. No matter which way you walk you sooner or later come to the foreshore and landmarks are visible from any point on the island. You can stop to refresh at one of the numerous street cafes that sell strong Italian coffee, traditional and delicious Cannoli or Tiramisu, or just peruse the dozens of authentic Sicilian craft shops that specialise in handmade artefacts representing different legends of the Island. There is always the smell of the sea, the salt air that drifts in across this island sanctuary. This sea air, mixed with the smells of fish cooking and the relaxed laughter of locals greeting each other, the banter of street markets, cobbled streets empty of cars, imbues a quiet nostalgia for the past, for long, carefree days. It is worth coming to Ortygia for this alone.

The street in which our apartment is located has an almost hushed, romantic wistfulness. It is difficult to explain this somewhat vague feeling, but from the moment we arrive I feel like I am back in my earliest childhood, seeing the neighbourhood through a lens of innocent wonder, yet with a strange familiarity. The old Ortygian women, sitting in open doorways knitting and chatting to one another across a narrow street, a housewife shaking a dusty rug from an upstairs bedroom, an unseen radio playing soft, slow jazz while flies buzz lazily around us in the warm sea air. It is truly enchanting. Time slows and the wider world becomes further removed. Life here is a simple one, uncomplicated by the plague of modern, fast-paced city life, the latest fashions or corporate images. It is a life where people are content with their lot, do not yearn for what is beyond their reach, do not crave a different life, just accept their simple pleasures, finding comfort in their faith and their family and fulfilling their small role in the Island's endless history.

Our apartment is rustic and spacious with ocean views and neighbours close by on either side. It has two large bedrooms, a large living area, small but well-equipped kitchen, open plan bathroom and a rooftop terrace that looks out on an expanse of a mesmerising sea. We relax into the lounge and listen to the comforting noises of the street below. Our final destination is one that will postpone the demands of returning to our hectic lives and instead, allow us to reminisce about a time and a world that we had almost forgotten.

The weather in Ortygia, as throughout our stay in Italy, is unblemished. Temperatures are in the low to mid 20s Celsius and skies are an endlessly azure blue. The air is pollution free. Our apartment is a stone's throw to the waterfront – a stone's throw to everything really. Walking is the norm and we take to it with relish. As usual in Europe, the seafront is not what you would expect in Australia or the USA. There are not endless beaches of white sand and palm trees. Instead, there are fishing vessels, tour boats, small harbours and plenty of seaside bars, restaurants and even hotels. In better known tourist spots such as Taormina, the beaches are segmented into free and paid territories. The free space is small and usually at the least desirable end of the beach, without view or amenities. In this space you can do what you want, no-one cares. The paid section of the beach is crowded with line after line of deck chairs and umbrellas. You pay for these by the hour and then pay some more if you would like extra services, such as towels, sun-cream, drinks to be served, etc. It is all very regulated, even regimented and in the height of summer, sunbathers are crammed in next to one another like sardines, not what you would consider your ideal summer relaxation.

Is this a beach?
In Ortygia, the scene is quite different. Yes, there are the mandatory bars and restaurants. Hotels are absent, as are the high-end clothing shops and boutiques. Beaches are *not* tourist destinations here, and, in fact, it is rather difficult to locate an identifiable beach at all. It is not really a term that comes to mind when strolling along the seashore in Ortygia. What we *do* spot with considerable amusement on one of our morning strolls, are five locals in swimsuits attempting to sunbake on a tiny strip of uncomfortably sharp pebbles between a stone harbour wall and the incoming tide. Less than five metres away from these brave souls are several deep-sea fishing trawlers unloading their latest catch. The stench of engine diesel, which incidentally, is spreading an oily film across the water of this "private beach", together with an overpowering smell of fish, does

not really make for a sunbather's paradise. But here they are, toughing it out with determination to get the most out of this beautiful weather. None of the other locals appear to find their presence amusing. No one actually seems to notice them at all, so I gather it must be a fairly common practice.

The Slow Lane

Settling into the atmosphere of the island is easy and comforting, adjusting to its slow pace, the almost ghostly streets, and natural beauty that surrounds you. In the evenings we stroll along the seafront, watching locals and tourists at play, riding bicycles, drinking lager, strolling with a lover, fishing from the wharf or simply sitting and watching. Fishing boats are returning to harbour with their catches and we're treated to the most magnificent sunset of deep tangerines and scarlet reds, changing through a spectrum of shades as the sun recedes into a darkening ocean. The scene is captivating. We feel our adrenaline slow and bodies relax as we enter a state of catatonic happiness.

Ortygia is a place that you can settle into and simply become part of. It has no expectations of you, instead, allowing you to unwind and become part of its enduring, entrancing fabric. We venture into Ortygia's Piazza Duomo at night to continue our meditation. The Piazza is large and oval in shape, surrounded by some of the most beautiful and iconic buildings of Sicily. The Baroque Cathedral, the Palace, and the Saint Lucia alla Badia Church and the grand Town Hall all look down on the Piazza in their imposing majesty, providing the scene with a regal atmosphere. The Piazza dates back to 800BCE and for almost three thousand years has been a sacred centre of worship as well as a gathering place for the weary after a long day. Today, the Piazza is lined with cafes and bars and is very much a place of the people.

At night, the ancient buildings are floodlit in a range of colours that create dreamy backdrops, adding to the relaxed mood. It is here that both Plato and Archimedes found solace, absorbing the same serenity that we do tonight. As Cicero himself commented; "(this is) ... the greatest Greek city and the most beautiful of them all". Locals agree. Tonight, with us, they are on their evening passeggiata, chatting to one another, drinking at bars, laughing together, being their Sicilian selves. It is the rhythm of the night, the unhurried tenor that appeals so much.

Ortygia is our last destination in Sicily and our evening in the Piazza, also one of our last. This 1950's sanctuary, and the ethereal beauty of this night in particular, resonate deeply. Wendy and I stand, holding hands, watching, absorbing the ambiance, the mood of the people, the subdued light, savouring the moment. Our mood swings from sadness to a meditative appreciation of what surrounds us. We have loved our time here. We love that a place like this still exists and thrives in a world so different. We love that here we can simply *be*.

Arrivederci

And so, we farewell our beloved Italy. Tomorrow we head to the UK, a story for another time. But for now, we can only reflect upon our time in this country as one of pure seduction. Wendy had been to Italy previously and already fallen in love once. I came with few expectations, believing at best, that it would be a tolerable prelude to our UK expedition.

Italy has turned out to be anything but a prelude. It has been a journey filled with romance, with wonder, with pure, unadulterated delight. To travel through a country, so striking in its beauty, its sense of history and culture, the passion of its people, is one of life's great pleasures. To do so with the person you love is an experience I will never forget.

Made in United States
Orlando, FL
13 December 2024

55575545R00057